MW00788425

AP PSYCHOLOGY PRACTICE EXAMS

SPARK NOTES™

SPARK PUBLISHING

AP exams and explanations written by David Cason.
Study cards written by Deborah Whitlow.
SparkChart written by Jennifer Cutler Stefani and Karen Schrier.

Spark Publishing
120 Fifth Avenue
New York, NY 10011
www.sparknotes.com

ISBN 1-4114-0487-4

Please submit changes or report errors to www.sparknotes.com/errors

Printed and bound in China.

CONTENTS

ACKNOWLEDGMENTS

SparkNotes would like to thank the following writers and contributors:

David M. Cason, Ph.D.
AP Psychology teacher, Troup High School, LaGrange, Georgia; AP Psychology Exam reader

Donna J. Dahlgren, Ph.D.
Associate professor of Psychology, Indiana University Southeast; AP Psychology Exam reader; AP exam development committee member

Karen Schrier

Jennifer Cutler Stefani

Deborah Whitlow, BA Psychology
AP Psychology, Calculus, and Literature teacher, Two Rivers School District, Plainview, Arkansas

INTRODUCTION

If you're looking at this book, you're probably at least considering taking the Advanced Placement Psychology Exam. And there are many good reasons to do so: AP exams give you the opportunity to earn valuable course credit or advanced standing in college, as well as the opportunity to impress on college admissions officers that you are a serious and dedicated student. AP exams offer one of the few chances to *prove* to colleges that you are already capable of doing college-level work.

In fact, the AP exams have become so highly touted, surrounded by so many expectations about what they say about you and what they can do for you, that it's easy for you to become overwhelmed or intimidated. We're here to tell you that the exam is manageable. We're here to help.

Practice exams are one of the very best ways to study for the AP exams, because they take away some of the mystique and hype regarding the exams and allow you to get comfortable with what's actually on the test. More important, they can help you understand what's *not* on the exam, so you don't waste your time striving for some elusive ideal of "college-level preparation." Practice exams will help you see the test as it really is, so you know exactly what to expect.

Before launching right into the exams, we'll give you an overview of how the test is structured and precisely what kinds of questions you'll see on it.

FORMAT OF THE EXAM

The Advanced Placement Psychology Exam is two hours long and is divided into two parts:

- A 70-minute multiple-choice section, which counts for 66 2/3 percent of your score
- A 50-minute free-response section, which counts for 33 1/3 percent of your score

The Multiple-Choice Section

Format

Section I of the exam contains 100 multiple-choice questions, which you are given 70 minutes to complete. The questions test your knowledge of material usually covered in an introductory psychology course in college.

The multiple-choice questions are either questions or incomplete statements, followed by five suggested answers or completions. The exam-graders penalize you a quarter-point for each wrong answer, so you should guess only if you can eliminate two or more of the answer choices.

Topics Tested on the Exam

The multiple-choice questions on the psychology exam will cover material that is generally taught in an introductory level psychology course in college. All multiple-choice questions will fall into one of fourteen topics, each of which is broken down into subtopics.

Each topic and subtopic is emphasized differently on the exam, which means that there will be more questions on some areas than on others. Here are the topics, the subtopics in each, and the approximate number of questions you'll find on each subject area on the exam:

TOPIC	SUBTOPIC	# OF QUESTIONS ON EXAM
History and Approaches	1. Logic, Philosophy, and History of Science 2. Types of Approaches	2–4
Research Methods	1. Experimental, Correlational, and Clinical Research 2. Statistics 3. Ethics	6–8
Biological Bases of Behavior	1. Physiological Techniques 2. Neuroanatomy 3. Nervous System 4. Neural Transmission 5. Endocrine System 6. Genetics	8–10
Sensation and Perception	1. Thresholds 2. Sensory Mechanisms 3. Sensory Adaptation 4. Attention 5. Perceptual Processes	7–9
States of Consciousness	1. Sleep and Dreaming 2. Hypnosis 3. Psychoactive Drug Effects	2–4
Learning	1. Classical Conditioning 2. Operant Conditioning 3. Cognitive Processes 4. Biological Factors 5. Social Learning	7–9
Cognition	1. Memory 2. Language 3. Thinking 4. Problem-Solving and Creativity	8–10
Motivation and Emotion	1. Biological Bases 2. Theories of Motivation 3. Hunger, Thirst, Sex, and Pain 4. Social Motives 5. Theories of Emotion 6. Stress	7–9

TOPIC	SUBTOPIC	# OF QUESTIONS ON EXAM
Development	1. Life-Span Approach 2. Research Methods 3. Heredity-Environment Issues 4. Developmental Theories 5. Dimensions of Development 6. Sex Roles and Differences	7–9
Personality	1. Theories and Approaches 2. Assessment Techniques 3. Self-Concept and Self-Esteem 4. Growth and Adjustment	6–8
Psychological Testing	1. Standardization and Norms 2. Reliability and Validity 3. Types of Tests 4. Ethics 5. Intelligence 6. Heredity/Environment and Intelligence 7. Diversity	5–7
Abnormal Psychology	1. Definitions 2. Theories 3. Diagnoses 4. Anxiety Disorders 5. Somatoform Disorders 6. Mood Disorders 7. Schizophrenic Disorders 8. Organic Disorders 9. Personality Disorders 10. Dissociative Disorders	7–9
Treatment of Psychological Disorders	1. Approaches 2. Types of Therapy 3. Community and Preventive Approaches	5–7
Social Psychology	1. Group Dynamics 2. Attribution Processes 3. Interpersonal Perception 4. Conformity, Compliance, Obedience 5. Attitudes and Attitude Change 6. Organizational Behavior 7. Aggression/Antisocial Behavior	7–9

As you can see, there are often more subtopics than there are questions, or more questions than there are subtopics. This makes it difficult to predict the exact content of the exam. There is a lot of material that might be covered, and not all of the material will make it on to every exam. The subtopics that are emphasized or overlooked change from year to year.

Though the topic areas are all equally important, you can see that some are emphasized more heavily than others on the test. The areas that are given the most questions on the exam are:

- Biological Bases of Behavior
- Cognition

The second-most emphasized topics are:

- Sensation and Perception
- Learning
- Motivation and Emotion
- Development
- Abnormal Psychology
- Social Psychology

The Free-Response Section

Types of Questions

Section II of the exam is a 50-minute free-response section made up of two questions. Each question will require you to display your knowledge of psychological concepts, terms, and research methods, as well as connect ideas from different areas of psychology in order to build a complete, nuanced answer. The questions you may be asked may include, but are not limited to, the following:

- Design a research study and discuss your strategies
- Analyze or critique a research study
- Evaluate a psychological problem using ideas from different realms of psychology
- Discuss various psychological terms or concepts and explain how they relate to a particular problem or idea

You should be sure to build a logical, complete answer and include only the information that is relevant to the question. You should avoid generalities and aim to provide specific information and examples that demonstrate your thorough knowledge of the topic at hand.

Scoring

Each free-response question is worth a different number of points depending on the type, difficulty, and breadth of the question. The questions and the scoring guidelines for each question are determined on a yearly basis, depending on the questions that will appear on the exam. In general, each question is worth 8–10 points, and points are earned for each element of the question that you address successfully.

SCORING

The AP exam is scored on a five-point scale:

5	Extremely well qualified
4	Well qualified
3	Qualified
2	Possibly qualified
1	No recommendation

HOW TO PREPARE FOR THE EXAM

The AP Psychology Exam tests your knowledge of material that generally makes up an introductory college course in psychology. You'll be tested on the major terms, theories, concepts, and approaches of psychology, and you'll be asked to apply psychological theories and methods to actual research problems and studies. In other words, you need to know the facts—as well as how to apply them to specific situations. A thorough understanding of psychology fundamentals is what the AP graders are looking for. You can increase your knowledge of psychology and deepen your understanding of how to apply psychological ideas by studying hard in your AP Psychology class and doing all the required reading.

To increase your ability to score high on the AP exam, the best thing you can do is take a lot of practice tests. That's why we've included two full-length tests in this book. The more familiar you are with the types of questions and the material they cover, the better you'll get at answering them. In the free-response section, the AP exam measures your ability to analyze, critique, and display knowledge of a more extensive concept or practical problem. You can improve your score in this section by practicing writing timed essays, focusing on including the most important information and structuring a logical, coherent response. The more familiar you are with the format of the exam, the better off you'll be on test day.

STRATEGIES FOR TAKING THE EXAM

Multiple-Choice Section

- Skim the questions first so you know what sorts of things you'll be reading for.
- Answer the questions you feel confident with first, skipping harder questions and saving them for last.
- Guess on questions when you can eliminate at least two wrong answers.
- Mark the questions you can't answer with a check—tackle all of these questions after you've gone through all of Section I.
- Cross off wrong answers on the test itself.

Free-Response Section

- Read the prompt carefully, underlining and marking the key parts of the question. Often the prompt gives you important pieces of guidance on purpose or on kinds of things to look for.
- Brainstorm ideas for your response, particularly the specific evidence you will use to support your ideas.
- Reread the prompt to make sure you haven't missed part of the question.
- Don't get hung up on perfect wording, spelling, etc.
- Don't just write down everything you can think of about the topic at hand. Be sure the information you include in your response is relevant to the question and organized clearly.
- If you run out of time, at least try and put down an outline of what you would liked to have written for the essay. You won't get full credit, but you may be able to pick up a point or two.

REGISTERING FOR THE EXAM

Contact your school's AP coordinator or guidance counselor for help registering for the test. If you are home-schooled or your school does not administer the test, contact AP Services for information about registering to take the exam at a school in your area that offers it.

AP Services
P.O. Box 6671
Princeton, NJ 08541-6671
(888) CALL 4AP; (609) 771-7300
TTY: (609) 882-4118
Email: apexams@ets.org
Website: www.collegeboard.com/ap/students/

PRACTICE EXAM 1

AP PSYCHOLOGY PRACTICE EXAM 1 ANSWER SHEET

1. Ⓐ Ⓑ Ⓒ Ⓓ Ⓔ	26. Ⓐ Ⓑ Ⓒ Ⓓ Ⓔ	51. Ⓐ Ⓑ Ⓒ Ⓓ Ⓔ	76. Ⓐ Ⓑ Ⓒ Ⓓ Ⓔ
2. Ⓐ Ⓑ Ⓒ Ⓓ Ⓔ	27. Ⓐ Ⓑ Ⓒ Ⓓ Ⓔ	52. Ⓐ Ⓑ Ⓒ Ⓓ Ⓔ	77. Ⓐ Ⓑ Ⓒ Ⓓ Ⓔ
3. Ⓐ Ⓑ Ⓒ Ⓓ Ⓔ	28. Ⓐ Ⓑ Ⓒ Ⓓ Ⓔ	53. Ⓐ Ⓑ Ⓒ Ⓓ Ⓔ	78. Ⓐ Ⓑ Ⓒ Ⓓ Ⓔ
4. Ⓐ Ⓑ Ⓒ Ⓓ Ⓔ	29. Ⓐ Ⓑ Ⓒ Ⓓ Ⓔ	54. Ⓐ Ⓑ Ⓒ Ⓓ Ⓔ	79. Ⓐ Ⓑ Ⓒ Ⓓ Ⓔ
5. Ⓐ Ⓑ Ⓒ Ⓓ Ⓔ	30. Ⓐ Ⓑ Ⓒ Ⓓ Ⓔ	55. Ⓐ Ⓑ Ⓒ Ⓓ Ⓔ	80. Ⓐ Ⓑ Ⓒ Ⓓ Ⓔ
6. Ⓐ Ⓑ Ⓒ Ⓓ Ⓔ	31. Ⓐ Ⓑ Ⓒ Ⓓ Ⓔ	56. Ⓐ Ⓑ Ⓒ Ⓓ Ⓔ	81. Ⓐ Ⓑ Ⓒ Ⓓ Ⓔ
7. Ⓐ Ⓑ Ⓒ Ⓓ Ⓔ	32. Ⓐ Ⓑ Ⓒ Ⓓ Ⓔ	57. Ⓐ Ⓑ Ⓒ Ⓓ Ⓔ	82. Ⓐ Ⓑ Ⓒ Ⓓ Ⓔ
8. Ⓐ Ⓑ Ⓒ Ⓓ Ⓔ	33. Ⓐ Ⓑ Ⓒ Ⓓ Ⓔ	58. Ⓐ Ⓑ Ⓒ Ⓓ Ⓔ	83. Ⓐ Ⓑ Ⓒ Ⓓ Ⓔ
9. Ⓐ Ⓑ Ⓒ Ⓓ Ⓔ	34. Ⓐ Ⓑ Ⓒ Ⓓ Ⓔ	59. Ⓐ Ⓑ Ⓒ Ⓓ Ⓔ	84. Ⓐ Ⓑ Ⓒ Ⓓ Ⓔ
10. Ⓐ Ⓑ Ⓒ Ⓓ Ⓔ	35. Ⓐ Ⓑ Ⓒ Ⓓ Ⓔ	60. Ⓐ Ⓑ Ⓒ Ⓓ Ⓔ	85. Ⓐ Ⓑ Ⓒ Ⓓ Ⓔ
11. Ⓐ Ⓑ Ⓒ Ⓓ Ⓔ	36. Ⓐ Ⓑ Ⓒ Ⓓ Ⓔ	61. Ⓐ Ⓑ Ⓒ Ⓓ Ⓔ	86. Ⓐ Ⓑ Ⓒ Ⓓ Ⓔ
12. Ⓐ Ⓑ Ⓒ Ⓓ Ⓔ	37. Ⓐ Ⓑ Ⓒ Ⓓ Ⓔ	62. Ⓐ Ⓑ Ⓒ Ⓓ Ⓔ	87. Ⓐ Ⓑ Ⓒ Ⓓ Ⓔ
13. Ⓐ Ⓑ Ⓒ Ⓓ Ⓔ	38. Ⓐ Ⓑ Ⓒ Ⓓ Ⓔ	63. Ⓐ Ⓑ Ⓒ Ⓓ Ⓔ	88. Ⓐ Ⓑ Ⓒ Ⓓ Ⓔ
14. Ⓐ Ⓑ Ⓒ Ⓓ Ⓔ	39. Ⓐ Ⓑ Ⓒ Ⓓ Ⓔ	64. Ⓐ Ⓑ Ⓒ Ⓓ Ⓔ	89. Ⓐ Ⓑ Ⓒ Ⓓ Ⓔ
15. Ⓐ Ⓑ Ⓒ Ⓓ Ⓔ	40. Ⓐ Ⓑ Ⓒ Ⓓ Ⓔ	65. Ⓐ Ⓑ Ⓒ Ⓓ Ⓔ	90. Ⓐ Ⓑ Ⓒ Ⓓ Ⓔ
16. Ⓐ Ⓑ Ⓒ Ⓓ Ⓔ	41. Ⓐ Ⓑ Ⓒ Ⓓ Ⓔ	66. Ⓐ Ⓑ Ⓒ Ⓓ Ⓔ	91. Ⓐ Ⓑ Ⓒ Ⓓ Ⓔ
17. Ⓐ Ⓑ Ⓒ Ⓓ Ⓔ	42. Ⓐ Ⓑ Ⓒ Ⓓ Ⓔ	67. Ⓐ Ⓑ Ⓒ Ⓓ Ⓔ	92. Ⓐ Ⓑ Ⓒ Ⓓ Ⓔ
18. Ⓐ Ⓑ Ⓒ Ⓓ Ⓔ	43. Ⓐ Ⓑ Ⓒ Ⓓ Ⓔ	68. Ⓐ Ⓑ Ⓒ Ⓓ Ⓔ	93. Ⓐ Ⓑ Ⓒ Ⓓ Ⓔ
19. Ⓐ Ⓑ Ⓒ Ⓓ Ⓔ	44. Ⓐ Ⓑ Ⓒ Ⓓ Ⓔ	69. Ⓐ Ⓑ Ⓒ Ⓓ Ⓔ	94. Ⓐ Ⓑ Ⓒ Ⓓ Ⓔ
20. Ⓐ Ⓑ Ⓒ Ⓓ Ⓔ	45. Ⓐ Ⓑ Ⓒ Ⓓ Ⓔ	70. Ⓐ Ⓑ Ⓒ Ⓓ Ⓔ	95. Ⓐ Ⓑ Ⓒ Ⓓ Ⓔ
21. Ⓐ Ⓑ Ⓒ Ⓓ Ⓔ	46. Ⓐ Ⓑ Ⓒ Ⓓ Ⓔ	71. Ⓐ Ⓑ Ⓒ Ⓓ Ⓔ	96. Ⓐ Ⓑ Ⓒ Ⓓ Ⓔ
22. Ⓐ Ⓑ Ⓒ Ⓓ Ⓔ	47. Ⓐ Ⓑ Ⓒ Ⓓ Ⓔ	72. Ⓐ Ⓑ Ⓒ Ⓓ Ⓔ	97. Ⓐ Ⓑ Ⓒ Ⓓ Ⓔ
23. Ⓐ Ⓑ Ⓒ Ⓓ Ⓔ	48. Ⓐ Ⓑ Ⓒ Ⓓ Ⓔ	73. Ⓐ Ⓑ Ⓒ Ⓓ Ⓔ	98. Ⓐ Ⓑ Ⓒ Ⓓ Ⓔ
24. Ⓐ Ⓑ Ⓒ Ⓓ Ⓔ	49. Ⓐ Ⓑ Ⓒ Ⓓ Ⓔ	74. Ⓐ Ⓑ Ⓒ Ⓓ Ⓔ	99. Ⓐ Ⓑ Ⓒ Ⓓ Ⓔ
25. Ⓐ Ⓑ Ⓒ Ⓓ Ⓔ	50. Ⓐ Ⓑ Ⓒ Ⓓ Ⓔ	75. Ⓐ Ⓑ Ⓒ Ⓓ Ⓔ	100. Ⓐ Ⓑ Ⓒ Ⓓ Ⓔ

AP PSYCHOLOGY
SECTION I
Time—1 hour and 10 minutes

100 Questions

<u>Directions:</u> Each of the questions or incomplete statements below is followed by five suggested answers or completions. Select the one that is best in each case and then fill in the corresponding oval on the answer sheet.

1. The system that controls voluntary muscle movement is called the

   (A) sympathetic nervous system
   (B) somatic nervous system
   (C) autonomic nervous system
   (D) parasympathetic nervous system
   (E) peripheral nervous system

2. Drive reduction theory focuses on the needs of individuals to maintain homeostasis. Which of the following is NOT an example of homeostasis?

   (A) Regulation of glucose levels in the blood
   (B) The maintenance of body temperature
   (C) The push and pull of external incentives
   (D) Both A and C are not examples of homeostasis
   (E) All are examples of homeostasis

3. Dwayne is nervous about an upcoming test. He makes the following statement: "My life will be ruined if I don't make an A+ on this test!" What would a therapist using rational emotive behavior therapy say or do in response to his statement?

   (A) The therapist would say Dwayne's id is intruding on his thoughts.
   (B) The therapist would say Dwayne needs to be systematically desensitized to his fear of tests.
   (C) The therapist would say Dwayne is aversively conditioned to test taking.
   (D) The therapist would directly challenge Dwayne's unrealistic and irrational thoughts.
   (E) The therapist would try to paraphrase and clarify Dwayne's statement about his grade.

4. Which of the following correctly traces the path of light rays as they enter the eye?

   (A) Cornea–lens–pupil–optic nerve–fovea
   (B) Retina–lens–cornea–optic nerve
   (C) Lens–pupil–optic nerve–retina
   (D) Cornea–pupil–lens–retina–optic nerve
   (E) Pupil–retina–lens–fovea–optic nerve

5. The rules for combining words into sensible sentences in a language are

   (A) morphemes
   (B) phonemes
   (C) grammar
   (D) syntax
   (E) semantics

6. Robert notes that his elderly grandmother seems to be a storehouse of wisdom and knowledge, but she often has difficulty reasoning and solving problems as quickly as she used to. This could be because

   (A) she has entered Freud's latency stage
   (B) her crystallized intelligence has increased, but her fluid intelligence is decreasing
   (C) she is a preconventional thinker
   (D) she needs to reset her social clock
   (E) she is in the concrete operational stage of development

7. Deena is searching for a new coat. In one store the coat was originally $150 but has been marked down to $100. In the second store, a similar coat is $100 but is not on sale. Deena goes back to the first store to purchase the coat. When asked why, she said that the first coat was a better deal because she saved $50. This is an example of

   (A) gambler's fallacy
   (B) framing effect
   (C) confirmation bias
   (D) overconfidence
   (E) generalization

8. Sometimes individuals who are participating in a group activity work less than if they were participating by themselves. This is called

   (A) social loafing
   (B) group polarization
   (C) deindividualization
   (D) generalization
   (E) transference

GO ON TO THE NEXT PAGE

9. MAOI drugs are most often prescribed for which of the following conditions?

   (A) Clinical depression
   (B) Dissociative identity disorder
   (C) Anxiety disorders
   (D) Narcissistic personality disorder
   (E) Organic disorder

10. A simple sugar whose levels in the blood help regulate feelings of hunger and fullness is

    (A) sucrose
    (B) fructose
    (C) insulin
    (D) orexin
    (E) none of these

11. George wants to study recall and aging. He interviews a series of people over a period of thirty years and examines how they change over time. What method is Jake using?

    (A) Longitudinal
    (B) Clinical
    (C) Cross-sectional
    (D) Double-blind
    (E) Experimentation

12. Professor Jones notes that a student is sleeping in class during a lecture. The professor assumes the student is lazy and disrespectful. This assumption would be an example of

    (A) transference
    (B) groupthink
    (C) deindividuation
    (D) dispositional attribution
    (E) self-serving bias

13. Two disciplines influenced the founding of psychology. The discipline that is a branch of biology and studies structures and functions of living organisms is _____; the discipline that concerns itself with mind-body dualism and nature-nurture issues is _____.

    (A) chemistry; physics
    (B) neurology; sociology
    (C) physics; neurology
    (D) physiology; philosophy
    (E) alchemy; philosophy

14. Ralph has been focusing on a particularly tough problem for days when all of a sudden he has a realization to the solution. What has Ralph just experienced?

    (A) Functional fixedness
    (B) Mental set
    (C) Prototypes
    (D) Fundamental attribution
    (E) Insight

15. On a farm, young chicks often follow the first thing they see that moves. This happens during the critical period. This process is called

    (A) imprinting
    (B) recapitulation
    (C) conditioning
    (D) assimilation
    (E) adjustment

16. All of the following are true of the Zimbardo Stanford prison experiment EXCEPT

    (A) ordinary college students were randomly assigned as prisoners or guards
    (B) some prisoners experienced emotional and physical ailments
    (C) the study was stopped early because of the danger to the prisoners
    (D) many of the guards were upset the study ended early
    (E) only guards with a history of violent behavior became aggressive toward the prisoners

17. June wants to lose weight. She has read about a miracle diet that claims to burn fat while she is asleep. What is the ad purporting to do?

    (A) Maintain homeostasis in her body
    (B) Provide extrinsic motivation
    (C) Reduce her instinct for food
    (D) Raise her basal metabolic rate
    (E) None of these

18. Which of these does NOT help explain humans' ability to perceive pitch?

    (A) Sensorineural conductivity
    (B) Place theory
    (C) The concept of the traveling wave within the cochlea
    (D) Frequency theory
    (E) Volley principle

GO ON TO THE NEXT PAGE

19. All of the following are true about Asch's conformity experiments EXCEPT

    (A) the larger the group, the more pressure there is to conform
    (B) the more insecure or incompetent a person is made to feel, the more likely he or she is to conform
    (C) the pressure to conform is greatest when the rest of the group is unanimous
    (D) if a person's behavior can be observed by others in the group, the more likely that person is to conform
    (E) all are true

20. When newborns are touched on the cheek, they often respond by demonstrating the

    (A) habituation response
    (B) accommodation reflex
    (C) rooting reflex
    (D) generalization response
    (E) formal operational stage

21. All of the following are true of the *Diagnostic and Statistical Manual for Mental Disorders IV* (*DSM-IV*) EXCEPT

    (A) it is widely used to diagnosis disorders
    (B) it is produced by the American Psychiatric Association
    (C) it includes over 10,000 disorder subcategories
    (D) a diagnosis must often fit the *DSM-IV* model in order for an insurance company to pay for the therapy
    (E) all are true

22. According to the *DSM-IV*, a psychological disorder that is distressing but allows a person to think rationally and function in society is called what?

    (A) Catatonic disorder
    (B) Psychotic disorder
    (C) Organic disorder
    (D) Neurotic disorder
    (E) Histrionic disorder

23. Which of the following theories of emotion states that our physiological arousal happens first, then we react with an emotion?

    (A) Cannon-Bard theory
    (B) James-Lange theory
    (C) Two-factor theory
    (D) Opponent-process theory
    (E) Drive-reduction theory

24. Donovan wants to wear the latest fashion so that he will fit in with his friends at school. He is experiencing

    (A) normative social influence
    (B) foot-in-the-door phenomenon
    (C) self-serving bias
    (D) bystander effect
    (E) cognitive dissonance

25. All of the following are neurotransmitters EXCEPT

    (A) adrenaline
    (B) dopamine
    (C) serotonin
    (D) acetylcholine
    (E) gamma-aminobutyric acid

26. Which of the following best describes drive-reduction theory?

    (A) Esteem needs will always be more important than safety needs
    (B) Motivations are often less important than instincts
    (C) Homeostasis cannot be achieved without optimal arousal
    (D) Psychological needs create an aroused tension state that motivates the organism to satisfy the need
    (E) Drives are met only when the organism understands motivations

27. The researcher most closely associated with psychosocial development and identity formation is

    (A) Piaget
    (B) Erikson
    (C) Bandura
    (D) Kohlberg
    (E) Skinner

28. Which theory of emotion states that the body attempts to adapt emotions to a level of homeostasis that is defined by prior experiences?

    (A) Cannon-Bard theory
    (B) James-Lange theory
    (C) Two-factor theory
    (D) Opponent-process theory
    (E) Drive-reduction theory

GO ON TO THE NEXT PAGE

29. Colby is conducting an experiment where he wants to discover if people can focus their attention on something to such a point that they do not notice routine background noises or other routine stimuli that might distract them. Which of these topics is Colby researching?

    (A) Transduction
    (B) Just noticeable difference
    (C) Sensory adaptation
    (D) Gestalt
    (E) Vestibular sense

30. At which stage of psychosocial development does a person work to refine a sense of self by testing roles?

    (A) Trust vs. mistrust
    (B) Autonomy vs. shame and doubt
    (C) Initiative vs. guilt
    (D) Identity vs. role confusion
    (E) Intimacy vs. isolation

31. Betty rationalizes that it is okay to steal a few dollars out of the cash drawer at work because her company is large and will never miss it. A few months later, her company announces it is being forced to enter bankruptcy because of high levels of employee theft, and Betty is among those who are laid off. Betty has experienced

    (A) a normative social influence
    (B) the foot-in-the-door phenomenon
    (C) self-serving bias
    (D) deindividuation
    (E) a social trap

32. Zachary is bilingual. He notices that when he speaks English, he thinks in English. When he speaks Spanish, he thinks in Spanish. Zachary has discovered

    (A) semantic encoding
    (B) linguistic relativity
    (C) morphemes
    (D) phonemes
    (E) syntactical encoding

33. The concept that people are not dissatisfied with their circumstances until they see someone else whom they perceive as having more than they do is called

    (A) generalization
    (B) relative deprivation
    (C) catharsis
    (D) subjective well-being
    (E) transference

34. All of the following statements are true concerning the normal curve in intelligence testing EXCEPT

    (A) 96 percent of scores fall within 30 points of 100
    (B) 68 percent of scores fall within 15 points of 100
    (C) extreme scores outnumber scores near the middle of the curve
    (D) the Flynn effect has been noted in every country that has been studied
    (E) we would expect a score of 130 plus to account for 2 percent of the population

35. Which of the following is NOT true about moral reasoning?

    (A) Just as with cognitive development, moral development involves stages
    (B) Kohlberg researched the stages of moral reasoning
    (C) The stages of moral reasoning are connected to the stages of cognitive development proposed by Piaget
    (D) Kohlberg proposed three stages of moral reasoning
    (E) Every adult eventually reaches the postconventional level of moral reasoning

36. Antipsychotic drugs such as Thorazine and Haldol are often used to treat schizophrenia and other psychoses. Antipsychotic drugs such as these are also called

    (A) SSRIs
    (B) MAOIs
    (C) tranquilizers
    (D) neuroleptics
    (E) tricyclics

37. All of the following are true of collectivist cultures EXCEPT

    (A) collectivist cultures prize harmony
    (B) collectivist cultures are almost always not as technologically advanced as individualistic cultures
    (C) collectivism increases a sense of connectedness
    (D) tradition far outweighs individual rights
    (E) society runs more smoothly when individuals know how to behave in a given situation

GO ON TO THE NEXT PAGE

38. Gene is required to take a test as part of a job interview process. He is told later that because of his scores on the test, they will be unable to hire him for the job. Gene goes on to take several other, similar jobs, and he fails at every one. What did the test mentioned here demonstrate?

    (A) Split-half reliability
    (B) Content validity
    (C) Criterion validity
    (D) Predictive validity
    (E) Test-retest reliability

39. Social security numbers and phone numbers are broken up into familiar number groups by dashes to ease memory. This is known as

    (A) serial position effect
    (B) semantic encoding
    (C) spacing effect
    (D) chunking
    (E) rehearsal

40. Which of the following psychologists is most closely associated with research into gender roles and connectedness?

    (A) Freud
    (B) Erikson
    (C) Piaget
    (D) Gilligan
    (E) Bandura

41. Which of the following does the visual cliff experiment demonstrate?

    (A) Form perception is more important than form sensation
    (B) Crawling babies possess depth perception
    (C) Selective attention can be learned
    (D) Brightness contrast causes our perception of color to change
    (E) Premonitions have genuine implications for psychology

42. What approach assumes that all behavior, normal or abnormal, is rooted in the interaction of nature and nurture?

    (A) Client-centered model
    (B) Biopsychosocial model
    (C) Medical model
    (D) Psychodynamic model
    (E) Humanistic model

43. Freud believed that because some memories were too painful to recall, the mind sometimes prevented their retrieval. This concept is known as

    (A) regression
    (B) transference
    (C) reappraisal
    (D) repression
    (E) none of these

44. According to modern explanations of dreaming, which of the following is NOT true?

    (A) Dreaming rarely occurs during NREM sleep
    (B) Dreams serve to sort and sift through a person's daily experiences
    (C) Dreams are the key to understanding and resolving inner conflicts
    (D) Neural activity during REM sleep provides periodic stimulation to the brain
    (E) Dreams are the mind's attempt to make sense of random neuron firing

45. Which of the following is true about the endocrine system?

    (A) The pituitary gland is the master gland of the endocrine system
    (B) The hypothalamus controls the pituitary gland
    (C) The adrenal glands are part of the endocrine system
    (D) The effects of the endocrine system on the body are slower than the effects of neurotransmitters but longer lasting
    (E) All are true

46. Social learning differs from classical conditioning because

    (A) classical conditioning is more long lasting than social learning
    (B) observation and modeling help explain behaviors that are not directly experienced
    (C) social learning cannot be as easily proved
    (D) classical conditioning better explains the effects of modeling
    (E) social learning occurs only in humans

GO ON TO THE NEXT PAGE →

AP PSYCHOLOGY MULTIPLE-CHOICE QUESTIONS

47. Imagine you've been studying for days for an important exam. When you finally take the exam, you panic because you're certain you've forgotten most of what you studied. Which of the following is most likely NOT the explanation for your failure to recall the information?

    (A) You've experienced *chunking*, the process of using abstract units of thought to represent a particular thing or quality
    (B) You've experienced *decay*, the fading away of memories over time
    (C) *Interference* may have occurred because you decided to read ahead into the next chapter just prior to the test
    (D) You've just experienced *repression*, in which access to information is blocked
    (E) You failed to move the information from short-term memory to long-term memory

48. Robin is attending a party and keeps moving from one group to another, listening to their conversations. Often referred to as the *cocktail party effect*, this is an example of

    (A) perceptual cues
    (B) perceptual adaptation
    (C) sensory deprivation
    (D) perceptual organization
    (E) selective attention

49. Gordon attended a performance of a noted hypnotist over the weekend. At work on Monday, he seems to be behaving strangely. Whenever someone calls his name, he barks like a dog. Which of the following concepts might best apply to his behavior?

    (A) Hypnotically refreshed memories
    (B) Social influence theory
    (C) Posthypnotic suggestion
    (D) Divided consciousness
    (E) Activation-synthesis model

50. What term refers to the measured intelligence of an individual compared to an average score for a person of the same age?

    (A) IQ
    (B) Mental age
    (C) General intelligence
    (D) Multiple intelligences
    (E) Factor analysis

51. Grover is in his eighties, yet he can recall in vivid detail where he was and what he was doing when he first heard about the attack on Pearl Harbor on December 7, 1941. This is an example of

    (A) flashbulb memory
    (B) sensory memory
    (C) working memory
    (D) long-term memory
    (E) short-term memory

52. A therapist tells Paula that her id is dominating her behavior. Which of these psychologists is most associated with the concept of the id?

    (A) Freud
    (B) Erikson
    (C) Piaget
    (D) Gilligan
    (E) Bandura

53. Structures that interact with other such structures to transmit signals from receptors to effectors or from one region of the nervous system or the other are called

    (A) neurons
    (B) stem cells
    (C) cell bodies
    (D) myelin sheaths
    (E) neurotransmitters

54. According to Freud, which of these psychosexual stages would one expect an adult to be experiencing?

    (A) Genital
    (B) Phallic
    (C) Latency
    (D) Oral
    (E) Anal

55. Which of the following would be classified as a psychoactive drug?

    (A) Cocaine
    (B) Valium
    (C) Caffeine
    (D) Mescaline
    (E) All of the above

GO ON TO THE NEXT PAGE

AP PSYCHOLOGY MULTIPLE-CHOICE QUESTIONS

56. Joe is six years old. His mother becomes upset when Joe hits his four-year-old sister. When asked why he hit her, he says he saw a cartoon character hit someone. What might explain Joe's behavior?

    (A) Classical conditioning
    (B) Observational learning
    (C) Discrimination
    (D) Modeling
    (E) Both B and D

57. Which of these defense mechanisms involves banishing anxious thoughts, feelings, and memories from the conscious?

    (A) Repression
    (B) Reaction formation
    (C) Rationalization
    (D) Generalization
    (E) Sublimation

58. A study was designed to test the effects of caffeine on sleep patterns. Group 1 was given regular coffee to drink just prior to bedtime. Group 2 was given decaffeinated coffee to drink. Which of the following is true?

    (A) Group 1 is the experimental group
    (B) Group 2 is the experimental group
    (C) Both groups are placebo control groups
    (D) Group 1 is the control group
    (E) Group 2 is more likely to quit the study

59. Personality inventories are often used to assess individuals in which of the following personality approaches?

    (A) Psychodynamic
    (B) Psychoanalytic
    (C) Trait
    (D) Humanistic
    (E) Social-cognitive

60. Which of the following monocular cues would an automobile manufacturer interested in constructing brighter illumination headlights for foggy driving situations be most concerned about?

    (A) Relative clarity
    (B) Interposition
    (C) Relative size
    (D) Relative motion
    (E) Texture gradient

61. Which of these arouses the body for defensive action?

    (A) Sympathetic nervous system
    (B) Somatic nervous system
    (C) Autonomic nervous system
    (D) Parasympathetic nervous system
    (E) Peripheral nervous system

62. What must a person have in order to overcome a sense of helplessness that is associated with the repeated occurrence of negative events?

    (A) Learned helplessness
    (B) Personal control
    (C) Introspection
    (D) Reciprocal determinism
    (E) External locus of control

63. Which of these would NOT be an example of the effective use of punishment?

    (A) An adolescent diagnosed with antisocial personality disorder is repeatedly spanked
    (B) A student who stops studying is ridiculed by friends
    (C) A worker's pay is docked because he arrives late for work
    (D) A person oversleeps and misses a bus to work
    (E) A student stops studying because it decreases the time she spends with her friends

64. According to Freud, the latent content of a dream is

    (A) the distinctive brain wave pattern of REM sleep
    (B) the previous day's events that caused the dream
    (C) the sensory stimuli experienced during sleep that stimulated the dream
    (D) the underlying but censored meaning of the dream
    (E) related to the perceptual consistency of the dream

65. In what projective testing method does a subject reveal inner feelings and interests through stories he or she creates about pictures of ambiguous scenes?

    (A) MMPI
    (B) Thematic Apperception Test
    (C) Stanford-Binet
    (D) Myers-Briggs
    (E) None of these

GO ON TO THE NEXT PAGE

AP PSYCHOLOGY MULTIPLE-CHOICE QUESTIONS

66. Bill likes to have students create graphic organizers of concepts they are learning in his class. He instructs them to create a graphical representation of how they link the major components of the concept in their mind. This is an example of a(n)

    (A) scattergram
    (B) cognitive map
    (C) operant typography
    (D) schedule of reinforcement
    (E) none of these

67. William notes that he seems to score well on both verbal and spatial reasoning portions of an intelligence exam. His revelation would support the concept of general intelligence, *g*. Which researcher is most associated with *g*?

    (A) Piaget
    (B) Spearman
    (C) Erikson
    (D) Binet
    (E) Terman

68. What is the basic difference between fMRI and MRI imaging techniques?

    (A) fMRI allows for real-time observations of changes in blood flow
    (B) MRI carries less risk for the patient
    (C) fMRI is more primitive and provides less detail
    (D) MRI is less invasive
    (E) Neither shows soft tissue structures as well as x-rays

69. Students are assigned the task of flipping a coin 50 times and recording the results. Assuming that heads (H) and tails (T) were each observed 25 times, which of the following would be the most likely sequence of heads and tails for the next 5 coin flips?

    (A) HHHHH
    (B) TTTTT
    (C) THTHT
    (D) HHTTH
    (E) All of the above would be equally likely

70. What type of mental disorder manifests itself with bizarre and irrational ideas, loss of contact with reality, and distorted perceptions?

    (A) Catatonic
    (B) Psychotic
    (C) Organic
    (D) Neurotic
    (E) Histrionic

71. Julie is expecting an important e-mail from her boyfriend, so she checks her e-mail several times during the day. What schedule of reinforcement applies to this situation?

    (A) Continuous
    (B) Variable interval
    (C) Fixed ratio
    (D) Fixed interval
    (E) Variable ratio

72. The full set of genes in each cell of an organism is known as the

    (A) chromosome
    (B) dendrite
    (C) genome
    (D) axon
    (E) nucleotide

73. Haley has become so worried about germs that she refuses to shake hands with people and washes her hands so often that her hands sometimes bleed. Which of these would be the diagnosis for Haley?

    (A) Panic disorder
    (B) Phobic disorder
    (C) Obsessive-compulsive disorder
    (D) Generalized anxiety disorder
    (E) Major depressive disorder

74. Which of the following are generally true about absolute threshold for the average person?

    (A) In a quiet room, a person can hear a watch ticking twenty feet away
    (B) Standing on a mountain in total darkness, a person can see a single candle thirty miles away
    (C) A person can feel the wing of a bee fall on his or her cheek
    (D) Both A and C
    (E) All of the above

75. Ariel is told that there is no medical explanation for her symptoms of physical discomfort. She is told that her pain and discomfort "must be in her head." What would be an appropriate diagnosis for Ariel?

    (A) Post–traumatic stress disorder
    (B) Phobic disorder
    (C) Obsessive-compulsive disorder
    (D) Generalized anxiety disorder
    (E) Somatoform disorder

GO ON TO THE NEXT PAGE

76. All of the following are true of Skinner's theories of operant conditioning EXCEPT

   (A) secondary reinforcers acquire their effect by association with other reinforcers
   (B) negative punishment is worse than positive punishment
   (C) a neutral consequence has no effect on the probability a response will reoccur
   (D) punishment weakens the response or makes it less likely to reoccur
   (E) reinforcement strengthens the response or makes it more likely to reoccur

77. For a person to be classified as having a psychological disorder, his or her behavior must be all of the following EXCEPT

   (A) disruptive
   (B) atypical
   (C) disturbing
   (D) maladaptive
   (E) unjustifiable

78. Glenn alternates between periods of wild optimism and deep depression. During his up periods he is reckless and extremely talkative. During his down periods he is morose and lethargic. Glenn seems to be afflicted with

   (A) seasonal affective disorder
   (B) dysrhythmic disorder
   (C) hypochondriasis
   (D) narcissistic personality disorder
   (E) bipolar disorder

79. The brain's higher-thinking and processing center, which consists of an intricate fabric of interconnected neural cells, is called the

   (A) corpus callosum
   (B) cerebral cortex
   (C) amygdala
   (D) medulla
   (E) cerebellum

80. Robert has been the victim of a telephone scam in which he lost some money. Now he is careful never to give out personal information over the telephone when someone asks for it. What term best describes what has happened to Robert?

   (A) Negative punishment
   (B) Negative reinforcement
   (C) Positive punishment
   (D) Positive reinforcement
   (E) Generalization

81. Which of these would be an example of instinctual drift?

   (A) Pigeons being trained by Skinner to play Ping-Pong
   (B) Children's biological disposition to learn language
   (C) Pavlov's dogs salivating at the sound of a bell
   (D) Watson's conditioning of "Little Albert" to fear small furry animals
   (E) None are examples

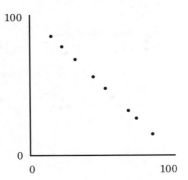

82. Examine the scatter plot above. What can you infer from the data on this graph?

   (A) Three variables have been placed on this graph
   (B) An almost perfect negative correlation exists
   (C) An almost perfect positive correlation exists
   (D) The two variables on the graph have no relationship
   (E) Only an illusory correlation exists

83. What portion of the brain includes the visual areas, which receive visual information from the opposite visual field?

   (A) Frontal lobe
   (B) Parietal lobe
   (C) Occipital lobe
   (D) Medulla
   (E) Cerebellum

GO ON TO THE NEXT PAGE

AP PSYCHOLOGY MULTIPLE-CHOICE QUESTIONS

84. Denise has been diagnosed with narcissistic personality disorder. Which of these best describes her?

   (A) She has a rigid, maladaptive personality pattern that causes her not to get along with others
   (B) She has intense but unstable relationships and fears abandonment
   (C) She lies, steals, and manipulates others and shows lack of guilt
   (D) She has an exaggerated sense of self-importance and self-absorption
   (E) She exhibits delusional behavior associated with hallucinations

85. What approach to psychotherapy attributes thoughts and actions to unconscious motives and conflicts?

   (A) Psychoanalysis
   (B) Humanistic
   (C) Behavioral
   (D) Eclectic
   (E) Biological

86. Variables in experimental design that interfere with the assignment of cause and effect are called

   (A) conflicting variables
   (B) compounding variables
   (C) competing variables
   (D) confounding variables
   (E) conspicuous variables

87. What would the double-blind procedure be most likely to minimize for both the participants and the researchers?

   (A) Random assignment
   (B) Replication
   (C) Observational definitions
   (D) Effects of expectations
   (E) Standard deviations

88. What kind of tests are designed to measure what someone has learned?

   (A) Intelligence
   (B) Aptitude
   (C) Achievement
   (D) Criterion referenced
   (E) Creativity

89. Researchers often find that extrinsic forces motivate behavior. Which of the following would be considered an extrinsic force?

   (A) Motivation
   (B) Instinct
   (C) Drive
   (D) Incentive
   (E) Hunger

90. Joey is in a hurry, and he is trying to locate milk in an unfamiliar grocery store. He decides to browse the store until he locates the dairy section, where he guesses the milk will be. Which of these best describes this problem-solving approach?

   (A) Concept
   (B) Prototype
   (C) Algorithm
   (D) Insight
   (E) Heuristic

91. Self-esteem would be most associated with which of the following perspectives?

   (A) Psychodynamic
   (B) Psychoanalytic
   (C) Trait
   (D) Humanistic
   (E) Social-cognitive

92. Which of the following perspectives emphasizes how people's thoughts and explanations affect their actions, feelings, and choices?

   (A) Behavioral
   (B) Social-cultural
   (C) Cognitive
   (D) Psychodynamic
   (E) Humanism

93. What approach assumes that psychopathy is an illness and should be diagnosed and treated like other illnesses?

   (A) Client-centered model
   (B) Biopsychosocial model
   (C) Medical model
   (D) Psychodynamic model
   (E) Humanistic model

GO ON TO THE NEXT PAGE

AP PSYCHOLOGY MULTIPLE-CHOICE QUESTIONS

94. Susan wants to teach her toddler how to use a spoon and fork correctly at the table when eating. At first, she shows her son the proper way to use a spoon and fork. Later, she continues to praise and reward him as he makes more and more attempts to use them properly. As time goes on, she requires more precise use on his part before he gets his praise and reward. After a few months, he uses a spoon and fork correctly without being told to. Which of the following best explains how Susan has taught him the proper way to use the spoon and fork?

   (A) Shaping
   (B) Extinction
   (C) Instinctive drift
   (D) Generalization
   (E) Counterconditioning

95. Once a student has been labeled a "troublemaker" or "slow" by his teachers, it is often hard for the student to overcome that label even after doing well in school because of

   (A) belief persistence
   (B) belief bias
   (C) overconfidence
   (D) generalization
   (E) confirmation bias

96. Electroconvulsive therapy (ECT) is generally accepted today to treat which of the following conditions?

   (A) Severe depression
   (B) Schizophrenia
   (C) Alcoholism
   (D) Suicidal thoughts
   (E) ECT is no longer accepted treatment for any condition

Use the following data to answer the next three questions.

Student Grades in English 101	
Student	Semester Average
A	73
B	73
C	96
D	80
E	88

97. What is the mode score for this data set?

   (A) 88
   (B) 96
   (C) 80
   (D) 85
   (E) 73

98. What is the mean score for this data set?

   (A) 88
   (B) 96
   (C) 70
   (D) 82
   (E) 73

99. What is the median score for this data set?

   (A) 88
   (B) 96
   (C) 70
   (D) 85
   (E) 80

100. Which of the following methods of psychology would be biological in approach?

   (A) Studying a person's inner conflicts
   (B) Investigating the relationship of stress to psychological disorders
   (C) Investigating how cultural rules and values affect people's development
   (D) Studying environmental rewards and punishers that maintain or discourage specific behaviors
   (E) Evaluating the relationship of how people express themselves creatively to their perception of achieving their full potential

END OF SECTION I

IF YOU FINISH BEFORE TIME IS CALLED, YOU MAY CHECK YOUR WORK ON THIS SECTION.

DO NOT GO ON TO SECTION II UNTIL YOU ARE TOLD TO DO SO.

AP PSYCHOLOGY
SECTION II

Time—50 minutes
Percent of total grade—33 $\frac{1}{3}$

Section II consists of two questions that each make up half of the score for Section II. You must answer both questions, using about half your time for each question. If you have extra time at the end of the exam, you may work on your responses.

AP PSYCHOLOGY
SECTION II

Time—50 minutes
Percent of total grade—33 $\frac{1}{3}$

<u>Directions:</u> You have 50 minutes to answer BOTH of the following questions. It is not enough to answer a question by merely listing facts. You should present a cogent argument based on your critical analysis of the question posed, using appropriate psychological terminology.

1. Describe the role of each of these concepts in the process of perception. Be sure to give a specific example of each concept.

   A. Gestalt
   B. Perceptual set
   C. Motion perception
   D. Depth perception
   E. Context

GO ON TO THE NEXT PAGE

2.   Psychiatrists are faced with the sometimes difficult task of diagnosing and recommending treatment for a variety of psychological disorders. When presented with symptoms, the clinician must make an appropriate diagnosis that is consistent with the *DSM-IV*. Using the standard definitions of each of the following psychological disorders, give an example of each and discuss typical symptoms of each.

    A. Anxiety disorders
    B. Mood disorders
    C. Dissociative disorders
    D. Schizophrenic disorders
    E. Personality disorders

END OF EXAMINATION

PRACTICE EXAM 1: ANSWERS & EXPLANATIONS

Answer Key for Practice Exam 1

Number	Answer	Right	Wrong	Number	Answer	Right	Wrong	Number	Answer	Right	Wrong
1	B	___	___	35	E	___	___	68	A	___	___
2	C	___	___	36	D	___	___	69	E	___	___
3	D	___	___	37	B	___	___	70	B	___	___
4	D	___	___	38	D	___	___	71	B	___	___
5	D	___	___	39	D	___	___	72	C	___	___
6	B	___	___	40	D	___	___	73	C	___	___
7	B	___	___	41	B	___	___	74	E	___	___
8	A	___	___	42	B	___	___	75	E	___	___
9	A	___	___	43	D	___	___	76	B	___	___
10	E	___	___	44	C	___	___	77	A	___	___
11	A	___	___	45	E	___	___	78	E	___	___
12	D	___	___	46	B	___	___	79	B	___	___
13	D	___	___	47	A	___	___	80	A	___	___
14	E	___	___	48	E	___	___	81	E	___	___
15	A	___	___	49	C	___	___	82	B	___	___
16	E	___	___	50	B	___	___	83	C	___	___
17	D	___	___	51	A	___	___	84	D	___	___
18	A	___	___	52	A	___	___	85	A	___	___
19	A	___	___	53	A	___	___	86	D	___	___
20	C	___	___	54	A	___	___	87	D	___	___
21	C	___	___	55	E	___	___	88	C	___	___
22	D	___	___	56	E	___	___	89	D	___	___
23	B	___	___	57	A	___	___	90	E	___	___
24	A	___	___	58	A	___	___	91	D	___	___
25	A	___	___	59	C	___	___	92	C	___	___
26	D	___	___	60	A	___	___	93	C	___	___
27	B	___	___	61	A	___	___	94	A	___	___
28	D	___	___	62	B	___	___	95	A	___	___
29	C	___	___	63	A	___	___	96	A	___	___
30	D	___	___	64	D	___	___	97	E	___	___
31	E	___	___	65	B	___	___	98	D	___	___
32	B	___	___	66	B	___	___	99	E	___	___
33	B	___	___	67	B	___	___	100	B	___	___
34	C	___	___								

HOW TO CALCULATE YOUR SCORE

Section I: Multiple Choice

$$\underline{\qquad} - (\tfrac{1}{4} \times \underline{\qquad}) = \underline{\qquad} = \underline{\qquad}$$

| Number Correct (out of 100) | Number Wrong | Multiple-Choice Score | Weighted Section I Score (Do not round.) |

Section II: Free Response

Question 1 $\underline{\qquad}$ ×   2.5000   = $\underline{\qquad}$
             (out of 10)

Question 2 $\underline{\qquad}$ ×   2.5000   = $\underline{\qquad}$
             (out of 10)

$$\underline{\qquad} + \underline{\qquad} = \underline{\qquad}$$

| Question 1 Score | Question 2 Score | Weighted Section II Score (Do not round.) |

Composite Score

$$\underline{\qquad} + \underline{\qquad} = \underline{\qquad}$$

| Weighted Section I Score | Weighted Section II Score | Composite Score (Round to the nearest whole number.) |

Composite Score*	AP Grade	Interpretation
93–150	5	extremely well qualified
72–92	4	well qualified
53–71	3	qualified
34–52	2	possibly qualified
0–33	1	no recommendation

*Each year the Development Committee determines the formulas used to calculate the raw composite scores. The Chief Faculty Consultant determines how the composite scores fit into the 5-point AP scale.

SECTION I: MULTIPLE-CHOICE EXPLANATIONS

1.   **B**   Biological Bases of Behavior: Functional Organization of the Nervous System
The somatic nervous system is part of the peripheral nervous system. It controls voluntary movements of skeletal muscles. The other portion of the peripheral nervous system is the autonomic nervous system, which controls the self-regulated action of internal organs and glands.

2.   **C**   Motivation and Emotion: Biological Bases
The human body works to avoid both deficits and surpluses, which is the fundamental idea of homeostasis. The body has a natural tendency to maintain a balanced internal state.

3.   **D**   Treatment of Psychological Disorders: Treatment Approaches/Cognitive Approaches
Albert Ellis developed rational emotive behavioral therapy. This therapy focuses on the fact that many clients have unrealistic notions of what they must do. As a result, they become upset over things that may or may not be serious problems. This therapy works by directly challenging these unrealistic or irrational thoughts.

4.   **D**   Sensation and Perception: Sensory Mechanisms
Light rays enter the eye through the cornea, a transparent protector, then pass through the pupil, an adjustable opening. The iris, a highly reactive colored muscle, determines the pupil's size. Light then passes through the lens, a transparent structure that changes shape to focus the light, and moves on to the retina, which lines the back of the eyeball. From there, light-sensitive cells send this visual stimulation to the optic nerve, which carries the signal to the visual cortex of the brain.

5.   **D**   Cognition: Language
Syntax is the system of rules for the ordering of words in a sentence. All of these things, however, are part of the thousands of languages spoken on earth. Phonemes are the smallest basic sounds of a language. Morphemes are the smallest units of language that carry meaning. Grammar is the system of rules for a language.

6.   **B**   Developmental Psychology: Life-Span Approach
As a person ages, studies indicate that his or her accumulated knowledge base continues to expand. This base is called *crystallized intelligence*. However, at the same time, his or her reasoning and problem-solving intelligence, called *fluid intelligence*, decreases.

7.   **B**   Cognition: Thinking
Framing of an issue or decision can have a huge effect on decision making and judgment. Framing is the way an issue is posed. In this example, Deena saved $50. The fact that she "saved" money makes this seem like the better choice, even though there was ultimately no difference in price. The way the issue was framed made all the difference in her decision.

8.   **A**   Social Psychology: Group Dynamics
People who are working in a group sometimes work less than they would if they had to complete a task by themselves. This phenomenon is caused by a sense of anonymity a person feels in a group, which makes him or her feel less accountable. Also, a person in a group might see his or her contribution as dispensable, motivating them to work less.

9.   A   Treatment of Psychological Disorders: Biological Approaches
MAOI drugs (monoamine oxidase inhibitors) are most often prescribed for depression, obsessive-compulsive disorder, and bipolar disorder. These drugs work by boosting levels of norepinephrine and serotonin, which keeps the levels of serotonin higher. Lower levels of serotonin are often associated with mood disorders.

10.   E   Motivation and Emotion: Hunger, Thirst, Sex, and Pain
Glucose levels in the blood help regulate hunger. The hormone insulin regulates glucose. Diabetics have an inability to produce insulin and cannot regulate glucose levels on their own.

11.   A   Developmental Psychology: Research Methods
Longitudinal studies follow the same group of people over a certain time period. The question specifies that he interviewed a group of people over thirty years and examined how they changed over time. Cross-sectional studies attempt to answer questions by comparing people of different ages to one another—how the same group of people change over a period of time isn't part of this kind of study.

12.   D   Social Psychology: Attribution Processes
When observing the behavior of another person, it is natural to search for explanations and attribute a cause for the behavior. In this example, Professor Jones is using dispositional attributions to explain why the student is sleeping. Using dispositional attributions assumes that a character defect or trait is the cause of behavior. This assumption may not be true and could lead to the fundamental attribution error, which is the ignoring of situational influences on behavior.

13.   D   History and Approaches: Logic, Philosophy, and History of Science
The fields of physiology and philosophy have long investigated phenomena that are today associated with psychology. Aristotle, the noted Greek philosopher, theorized about learning and memory in the years around 300 B.C. Wilhelm Wundt, the founder of psychology, was both a philosopher and physiologist.

14.   E   Cognition: Thinking
Insights are sudden, novel solutions to problems. Insights differ from more methodical approaches to problem solving such as heuristics and algorithms. Functional fixedness and mental set hinder problem solving, and prototypes and fundamental attribution do not directly concern problem solving.

15.   A   Developmental Psychology: Heredity-Environment Issues
Imprinting is a rigid attachment process that usually takes place at a very early age. This period of imprinting is referred to as the critical period. Conditioning, assimilation, and adjustment are concepts related to learning, but none of these specifically concerns this intense bonding that occurs early in life. Recapitulation is not a psychological term applicable to this idea.

16.   E   Social Psychology: Conformity, Compliance, Obedience
Zimbardo's Stanford prison experiment is a classic in research on obedience. All of the statements in the answers to this question are true except for **E**. There was no relationship between past aggressive behavior and the behavior of the guards in this study. In fact, even the guards who did not become aggressive failed to intervene when they observed aggressive behavior.

17.   **D**   Motivation and Emotion: Hunger, Thirst, Sex, and Pain

Basal metabolic rate is a measure of the body's resting rate of energy expenditure. If the ad claims June will lose weight while she sleeps, then it must intend to raise her basal metabolic rate.

18.   **A**   Sensation and Perception: Sensory Mechanisms

Place theory assumes that we hear different pitches based on the area of the cochlea that is stimulated. It best explains the perception of high-pitched sounds. Researcher Gerog von Bekesy discovered that a traveling wave was present in the cochlea when sound was entering it. Frequency theory helps explain how people detect low pitches. The volley principle suggests that neural cells alternate firing so that people can perceive very high-pitched sounds.

19.   **A**   Social Psychology: Conformity, Compliance, Obedience

Asch's conformity experiment is a classic in conformity research. He discovered that the isolation of being a lone dissenter puts great social pressure on a person to conform. Surprisingly, a group of three puts just as much conformity pressure on a person as larger groups do.

20.   **C**   Developmental Psychology: Heredity-Environment Issues

The rooting reflex is the tendency for babies to search for the nipple when they are touched on the cheek. This seems to be a basic instinctual response to the baby's sense of hunger.

21.   **C**   Abnormal Psychology: Diagnosis of Psychopathology

The *DSM-IV* is the standard of diagnosis of mental disorders. All of these choices are true of the *DSM-IV* except for answer **C**—the *DSM-IV* includes around 400 subcategories of disorders, not 10,000.

22.   **D**   Abnormal Psychology: Diagnosis of Psychopathology

Neurotic disorders are disorders that can cause discomfort and distress while still allowing a person to think rationally and function in society. They do not cause irrational behavior or interfere with a person's ability to function in society as catatonic, psychotic, organic, or histrionic disorders might.

23.   **B**   Motivation and Emotion: Theories of Emotion

Emotions arise from the combination of physiological arousal, expressive behavior, and conscious experience. The James-Lange theory of emotion states that we first experience physiological arousal to a stimulus and then react to that physiological arousal with an emotion. This is similar to the two-factor theory, which stresses the importance of a cognitive label in helping people to interpret the physical arousal they're experiencing. The difference is that the two-factor theory presumes that emotions are physiologically similar, so a person must consciously "label" that physiological response. The Cannon-Bard theory suggests that the physiological arousal and the emotion occur at the same time and does not concern a cognitive label. The opponent-process theory proposes that every emotion brings with it the opposite emotion. The drive-reduction theory concerns motivation, not emotion.

24.   **A**   Social Psychology: Conformity, Compliance, Obedience

Normative social influence occurs when a person acts to either gain approval or avoid disapproval from a social group. In this example, Donovan's main reason for wanting to be fashionable is to gain acceptance from his social group.

25.   **A**   Biological Bases of Behavior: Neural Transmission

Neurotransmitters are the body's method of communicating between neurons. These chemical messengers are released from the vesicle of the sending neuron and bind with receptor sites on the receiving neuron. These chemical messengers unlock tiny channels in the receiving neuron, which then allow ions to enter and start the process of the action potential. Adrenaline is not a neurotransmitter. It is a hormone that is released into the bloodstream by the adrenal glands.

26.   **D**   Motivation and Emotion: Theories of Motivation

Originally, research in motivation focused on behavior being controlled by biological forces, often referred to as instincts. Later, research began to explore the concept of drives and incentives in behavior. The aim of drive reduction is internal stability, or homeostasis. Thus, drive reduction motivates certain survival behaviors. However, we are not only pushed by internal drives but also pulled by external incentives.

27.   **B**   Developmental Psychology: Developmental Theories

Erik Erikson was interested in the social development of individuals. He believed that each stage of life involved some type of crisis that must be resolved in order to move on to the next stage and that the resolution of these crises shaped identity.

28.   **D**   Motivation and Emotion: Theories of Emotion

Emotions arise from the combination of physiological arousal, expressive behavior, and conscious experience. The opponent-process theory of emotion says that every emotion produces an opposite emotion. For example, situations that produce fear can also produce elation. This theory helps explain why emotions tend to balance.

29.   **C**   Sensation and Perception: Sensory Adaptation

People who are exposed to constant, routine stimuli often notice these stimuli less and less as time goes on. Sensitivity diminishes in response to unchanging stimuli in a process called *sensory adaptation*. Sensory adaptation is one of the mental processes that help people focus their full attention on important tasks. People diagnosed with attention deficit disorder are often unable to filter out routine stimulations, which causes them to become more easily distracted than others.

30.   **D**   Developmental Psychology: Dimensions of Development/Social

Roles are associated with the identity vs. role confusion stage of adolescence, part of the theory of psychosocial development proposed by Erik Erikson. Erikson believed that each stage of life involved some type of crisis that must be resolved in order to move on to the next stage.

31.   **E**   Social Psychology: Aggression/Antisocial Behavior

Social traps occur when people pursue their own self-interests at the expense of another person. In this example, Betty takes the money without thinking about the possible negative effects her actions could have on the company. Normative social influence involves seeking approval from others, which Betty is not doing. The self-serving bias is the tendency for a person to view himself or herself favorably, but it has nothing to do with doing so at the expense of others. Deindividuation and the foot-in-the-door phenomenon concern influence and group behavior, and Betty is acting alone.

32.   **B**   Cognition: Language

Benjamin Whorf noted that specific differences in language are often found in the way people think and conceptualize ideas. He called this concept *linguistic relativity*. Linguistic relativity explains why literal translations of phrases in foreign languages often sound wrong or confusing.

33.   **B**   Motivation and Emotion: Stress

Relative deprivation is a person's perception that he or she is worse off physically, financially, or otherwise in comparison to others. An example of relative deprivation: some people who lived during the Great Depression claim that no one realized he or she was poor because everyone was poor.

34.   **C**   Testing and Individual Differences: Standardization and Norms

The normal curve is a symmetrical bell-shaped curve that describes a normal distribution of scores. As we move away from the middle of the curve, we would expect to find fewer and fewer scores. That is, as scores become more extreme, we find fewer of them. The most scores fall in the middle area of the curve. The Flynn effect is the recently noted phenomenon that worldwide intelligence test scores have been on the rise over the past seven or eight decades.

35.   **E**   Developmental Psychology: Dimensions of Development/Moral

Lawrence Kohlberg posed moral dilemmas to subjects to examine how they responded to and reasoned out these dilemmas. He identified three levels of moral development: the preconventional level, from birth to about age nine; the conventional level, from age nine to adolescence or early adulthood; and the postconventional level, which many people never attain. Much of his work was based on Piaget's stages of cognitive development. Not all adults reach the postconventional level, which many critics claim applies mostly to people in societies that value individual goals rather than communal goals.

36.   **D**   Treatment of Psychological Disorders: Treatment Approaches/Biological
         Approaches

Antipsychotic drugs are also called *neuroleptics*. Some neuroleptics operate by lowering levels of dopamine. Others operate by increasing levels of serotonin. These drugs work well to inhibit delusions and hallucinations, but they often worsen some symptoms such as jumbled thoughts and emotional flatness.

37.   **B**   Social Psychology: Organizational Behavior

Contrary to conventional wisdom, collectivist cultures are not always less technologically advanced. South Korea and Japan, two highly technologically advanced countries, have strong collectivist cultures.

38.   **D**   Testing and Individual Differences: Reliability and Validity

Predictive validity is the ability to predict future achievement. The intention of the company's test was to predict how Gene might perform on the job he was applying for. Though we can't know exactly how Gene would have performed on that particular job, the fact that he failed at several other similar jobs suggests that the test was accurate in suggesting Gene would not perform well. The test therefore demonstrated predictive validity, since the intention was to measure or predict future behavior, and it seemed to do so accurately. Validity is a measure of how well a test measures what it is supposed to.

39. **D** Cognition: Memory

Chunking is the organization of information into more easily remembered units. Often the mind does this automatically so that items are more easily remembered. Social security numbers are divided 111-11-1111 so that they are easier to recall—it's easier to remember three groups of three, two, and four numbers each than one group of nine numbers.

40. **D** Developmental Psychology: Sex Roles, Sex Differences

Carol Gilligan's research has focused on how men often struggle to create separate identities and women often are more interested in making connections. Her research indicates that men are more independent and women are more interdependent.

41. **B** Sensation and Perception: Sensory Adaptation

This classic experiment involved placing six- to fourteen-month-old infants in a laboratory device that simulated a cliff but in reality was covered with glass. Researchers found that infants who could crawl could not be coaxed across the glass. Further, they found that various newborn animals likewise refused to step off the solid ground. This indicated that most mobile animals seemed to possess the perceptual abilities they need for survival.

42. **B** Abnormal Psychology: Theories of Psychopathology

The biopsychosocial model assumes that a variety of nature and nurture factors form the basis of all behavior. These factors include genetic factors, stress, trauma, and cultural factors.

43. **D** Cognition: Memory

Freud believed that the mind often self-censored, or repressed, painful information in order to protect itself. He believed that this process is a basic survival drive. Repression is a defense mechanism, along with regression, which involves returning to a more infantile psychological state to cope with anxiety.

44. **C** States of Consciousness: Sleep and Dreaming

The belief that dreams are the key to understanding our inner conflicts is a Freudian concept that has been overshadowed by more recent research. Three modern theories of dreaming exist. Answer **B** describes the information-processing model of dreaming. Answer **D** describes the physiological function of dreaming, and answer **E** describes the activation synthesis model of dreaming.

45. **E** Biological Bases of Behavior: Endocrine System

The endocrine system is a group of organs and glands in the body that produce hormones. Hormones are chemical substances that are secreted by glands in the endocrine system. The purpose of these substances is to regulate the functions of other organs. Neurotransmitters are released in minute amounts and have near-instantaneous effects. Hormones are released in large amounts directly into the bloodstream and are slower to take effect, but they last longer.

46. **B** Learning: Social Learning

Social-cognitive theory investigates how behavior is learned through observation of others. Social learning occurs when an individual learns new responses by observing and modeling others' behavior.

47. **A** Cognition: Memory

Chunking is the process of grouping pieces of information for easier handling, so this would be linked to remembering, not forgetting. Forgetting may occur because of *decay*, which is the fading away of memory; *interference*, which occurs when new or old information blocks the memory of a related piece of information; or *repression*, which is when access to information has been blocked. Sometimes we can store small pieces of information in short-term memory. If that memory is not encoded into long-term memory, it will most likely be forgotten.

48.   **E**   Sensation and Perception: Attention
Because of the massive volume of stimuli we constantly encounter, our minds must filter this stimulation into usable information. As a result, we experience selective attention. Selective attention occurs when the mind focuses on only a limited number of manageable stimuli and ignores others, especially routine or lower-level stimuli.

49.   **C**   States of Consciousness: Hypnosis
Posthypnotic suggestion is the carrying out of a suggestion made by a hypnotist after hypnosis has ended. Research indicates that people with low susceptibility to suggestion might well follow through with these suggestions. However, studies indicate that the success rates for many therapies that use hypnosis are no greater than similar therapies that do not use hypnosis.

50.   **B**   Testing and Individual Differences: Intelligence
Mental age is a comparison of a person's score on an intelligence test to an average score for someone of the same age. If a person's mental age is the same as his or her chronological age, then the computed IQ would be 100. The mental age measurement works best for children.

51.   **A**   Cognition: Memory
Flashbulb memories are clear memories of emotionally significant events or moments. Flashbulb memories form because the mind determines that these types of events are of high priority and thus must be easily accessible and easily recalled.

52.   **A**   Personality: Personality Theories and Approaches
Freud believed the mind was made up of the conscious, the preconscious, and the unconscious, and he linked each type of consciousness with a particular psychological concept: the *id* is associated with the unconscious, the *ego* is associated with the conscious, and the *superego* is associated with the preconscious. The id operates on the pleasure principle, concerned only with satisfying its needs and desires. Freud believed that personality was formed primarily by the unconscious.

53.   **A**   Biological Bases of Behavior: Functional Organization of the Nervous System
Neurons, or nerve cells, are the basic building blocks of our nervous system. These specialized cells consist of a central cell body surrounded by dendrites, which receive neural stimulation. This information is then passed up the axon to other neurons, muscles, or glands. The neuron fires an electrical impulse when stimulated. This is known as the action potential. The average human body contains approximately 10 billion neurons.

54.   **A**   Personality: Personality Theories and Approaches
Freud saw personality development as a series of psychosexual stages. The oral stage lasts from birth to eighteen months. The anal stage lasts from eighteen to thirty-six months. The phallic stage lasts from three to six years. The latency stage lasts from six years until puberty. The genital stage lasts from puberty until adulthood. Freud theorized that each of

these stages represents the id's attempt to seek pleasure from different areas of the body called erogenous zones.

55. **E** States of Consciousness: Psychoactive Drug Effects
All of these drugs are classified as psychoactive because each one has the ability to alter perception, mood, thinking, memory, or behavior.

56. **E** Learning: Social Learning
In this question, Joe has observed an action on television and then imitated that behavior with his little sister. In effect, he learned a behavior from observing it on television—he learned by watching others. This type of process is called observational learning or modeling.

57. **A** Personality: Personality Theories and Approaches
Freud theorized that people's egos protect them from anxiety by employing defense mechanisms. Repression is a defense mechanism that involves pushing anxious thoughts, feelings, or memories out of the consciousness. The other defense mechanisms listed in this question handle anxiety differently. In reaction formation, the ego changes unacceptable impulses into their opposites. In rationalization, the ego justifies false reasons for actions to avoid facing real reasons. In sublimation, the ego changes unacceptable impulses into positive motivations. Generalization is not a defense mechanism.

58. **A** Research Methods: Experimental, Correlational, and Clinical Research
In order to determine if the caffeine does indeed affect sleep, there must be both a control and experimental group. Here, group 1 is the experimental group because they receive the caffeine, which is called the treatment. Group 2 receives only a placebo (decaffeinated coffee), which makes them the control group. This research design helps to determine whether the treatment does have an effect, and it helps to ensure that the results of the experiment are actually caused by the treatment and not by subjects' expectations.

59. **C** Personality: Personality Theories and Approaches
Personality inventories are questionnaires that normally ask people to respond to true/false or agree/disagree questions with the intention of discovering a wide range of behaviors. They are often utilized to identify personality traits.

60. **A** Sensation and Perception: Perceptual Processes
A number of monocular cues affect how a person judges distance. A headlight manufacturer would be most interested in relative clarity, which is the perception that the more hazy or distorted an object, the farther away it must be. In repeated studies of drivers in foggy conditions, drivers often had difficulty effectively judging distances. In fact, drivers are often lulled into accelerating in foggy conditions.

61. **A** Biological Bases of Behavior: Functional Organization of the Nervous System
The autonomic nervous system is composed of two parts: the sympathetic and parasympathetic nervous systems. The purpose of the sympathetic nervous system is to prepare the body for defensive action, also called the "fight-or-flight" reaction. The purpose of the parasympathetic nervous system is to calm the body to conserve energy.

62. **B** Personality: Personality Theories and Approaches

Learned helplessness often results when people have learned that regardless of what they might do, they are unable to avoid repeated negative events. This is the opposite of a sense of personal control, which people feel when they have a sense that they are able to control their environment.

63. **A** Learning: Biological Factors

Researchers have discovered that biological factors often constrain the limits of learning that can take place. In this example, all but choice **A** are examples of effective punishments, both positive and negative, that might change behavior. Research shows that people with some mental disorders, such as antisocial personality disorder, often fail to respond to punishment the way other people would.

64. **D** States of Consciousness: Sleep and Dreaming

Freud conceived of two components of dreaming: manifest content and latent content. *Manifest content* is the obvious storyline of the dream. *Latent content* is the hidden or underlying content of the dream. Freud believed the dreamer will self-censor or repress memories that are too painful and have no conscious memory of them. However, these memories can be seen in the latent content of the dreams.

65. **B** Personality: Assessment Techniques

The Thematic Apperception Test (TAT) asks subjects to describe what is happening in pictures of ambiguous scenes. The subjects' descriptions and stories will, in theory, reveal subjects' inner feelings and thoughts.

66. **B** Learning: Cognitive Processes in Learning

Cognitive maps are mental representations of how a person sees a concept or a problem. In this situation, Bill is asking the students to transfer their cognitive maps to paper so that he can better understand the students' thought processes.

67. **B** Testing and Individual Differences: Human Diversity

Charles Spearman, the developer of factor analysis, noted that people with strong intelligence in one area often score well in other areas of intelligence. He called this general intelligence, or *g*.

68. **A** Biological Bases of Behavior: Physiological Techniques

Magnetic resonance imaging (MRI) is a technique that provides highly detailed images of the brain using electromagnetic signals generated by the brain in response to magnetic fields. Functional MRI (fMRI) is a more advanced type of imaging that takes multiple images of the brain, which reveal minute changes in blood flow to parts of the brain. fMRI is, therefore a more advanced form of MRI, which allows researchers to observe changes in the brain during experimentation.

69. **E** Research Methods: Experimental, Correlational, and Clinical Research

The chances of the next coin flip being either heads or tails remains the same for every flip regardless of the last flip, so any of the answer choices here are equally possible. Students who believe they can "predict" the next flip based on the previous flip are exhibiting an illusory correlation, which is a perceived correlation that does not actually exist. When we believe, without scientific observation, that a relationship exists between two things, then we are more likely to notice and recall events that confirm our belief. In other words, students who believe in the connection between flips will be more likely to notice and remember the times when their prediction of the coin flip turned out to be correct. This idea helps to explain the persistence of superstitions. The attempt to perceive patterns even when they do not exist might explain the popularity of gambling and other games of chance.

70. **B**   Abnormal Psychology: Schizophrenic Disorders
One of the most distinguishing features of psychotic disorders is irrationality. Psychotic disorders are often characterized by disorganized and delusional thinking, disturbed perceptions, inappropriate actions and emotions, and a preoccupation with delusions and hallucinations. People suffering from psychotic disorders generally cannot function normally in society. Organic, neurotic, and histrionic disorders all typically allow a person to maintain rational thinking and function in society. Catatonic behavior is characterized by manic behavior or complete withdrawal.

71. **B**   Learning: Operant Conditioning
Julie expects that an e-mail will come at some point in the future, but she does not know the exact time, so she checks her e-email frequently. This is a variable-interval schedule of reinforcement because the reinforcement occurs after some unknown amount of time—an e-mail may arrive in the morning, or it may not arrive until late at night. The idea of a variable-interval reinforcement schedule was proposed by Skinner, who discovered that once a behavior is learned, the reinforcement of that learning could happen on various learning schedules.

72. **C**   Biological Bases of Behavior: Genetics
Genes are specific sequences of DNA molecules that are the functional units of heredity, and the *genome* is a blueprint for the entire genetic structure of a living organism. No other answer choices describe this full set of genes. DNA transfers genetic characteristics by way of coded instructions in the form of four nucleotide bases. Chromosomes are rodlike structures that contain genes. Dendrites and axons are parts of a nerve cell.

73. **C**   Abnormal Psychology: Anxiety Disorders
Obsessive-compulsive disorder is characterized by unwanted, repetitive thoughts and actions. This disorder is most common in teens and young adults. If the disorder becomes serious, a person can become controlled by these repetitive thoughts and actions.

74. **E**   Sensation and Perception: Thresholds
Surprising as it might seem, all of these are true. Absolute threshold is defined as the minimum stimulation needed to detect a given stimulus 50 percent of the time. In other words, the average person under ideal conditions should be able to accomplish all of these things half the time.

75. **E**   Abnormal Psychology: Somatoform Disorders
Somatoform disorders are psychological disorders that cause medically unexplainable symptoms. These disorders were often dismissed in the past as being fantasies in the mind of the patient.

76. **B**   Learning: Operant Conditioning
In operant conditioning, the terms "positive" and "negative" when describing punishment do not imply value judgments. Positive does not mean "good"; rather, it means that something is given. Negative does not mean "bad"; it means that something is taken away.

77. **A** Abnormal Psychology: Definitions of Abnormality

According to the APA, a person with a psychological disorder must exhibit behavior that is atypical, disturbing, maladaptive, and unjustifiable. This definition does not include disruptive behavior as a criterion for having a psychological disorder. Behavior that does not meet all of the criteria in this definition might be considered eccentric, but it would not signal a true psychological disorder.

78. **E** Abnormal Psychology: Mood Disorders

Bipolar disorder, once known as manic-depressive disorder, is a mood disorder in which a person alternates between periods of deep depression and overexcited mania. Bipolar disorder is much less common than depression and is found equally in both men and women.

79. **B** Biological Bases of Behavior: Neuroanatomy

The cerebral cortex is the ultimate control and processing center of the brain. This thin surface layer of cells one-eighth of an inch thick consists of over thirty billion nerve cells. All higher forms of thinking occur here. The other answer choices are also parts of the brain: the corpus callosum is a group of nerve fibers connecting the two halves of the brain, the amygdala regulates emotion, the medulla controls automatic functions, and the cerebellum controls movement and balance.

80. **A** Learning: Operant Conditioning

Robert has been punished by having his money taken away—he's experienced negative punishment. In operant conditioning, "positive" and "negative" do not suggest "good" and "bad." Rather, "positive" means that something is given, while "negative" means that something is taken away.

81. **E** Learning: Biological Factors/Instinctive Drift

Researchers have discovered that biological factors often constrain the limits of learning that can take place. This is called instinctual drift, which is the tendency to revert to instinctive behavior. All of the examples are situations where conditioning has occurred to create noninstinctive behavior.

82. **B** Research Methods: Statistics

A negative correlation means that two variables have an inverse relationship—as one variable goes up, the other goes down. When graphed, the line moves down and to the right, as the line does in this question. When the relationship between two variables is studied, one method of observing the strength of the relationship is to plot the values of the two variables on a graph known as a *scatter plot* or *scattergram*. A negative correlation is shown in this question. A positive correlation means that two variables relate to each other in direct proportion—as one goes up, the other goes up. When graphed, the line moves up and to the right. If two variables have no relationship, then the plotted points will be scattered about the graph in no discernable pattern.

83. **C** Biological Bases of Behavior: Neuroanatomy

The occipital lobe of the brain is located in the lower back portion of the cerebral cortex. Its primary function is to receive visual information via the optic nerve. This visual information is then processed in the visual cortex region of the occipital lobe. The other parts of the brain listed here do not relate to vision. The frontal lobe controls short-term memory, speech, and higher thinking; the parietal lobe processes temperature, touch, pain, and pressure; the medulla controls automatic functions; and the cerebellum controls movement and balance.

84. **D** Abnormal Psychology: Personality Disorders
Narcissistic personality disorder is characterized by a preoccupation with fantasies of one's own importance, power, and brilliance. People with this disorder often demand special favors and treatment but are unwilling to return those favors for others.

85. **A** Treatment of Psychological Disorders: Insight Therapies: Psychodynamic/ Humanistic Approaches
Psychoanalysis, which was developed by Freud, assumes that personality is like an iceberg: most of it is hidden. Much of the personality is in the unconscious, which is below the surface and not seen. A psychoanalytic therapist attempts to uncover those hidden causes of behavior by asking probing questions.

86. **D** Research Methods: Experimental, Correlational, and Clinical Research
Confounding variables in research design are unaccounted for or unanticipated variables that interfere with or prevent the assigning of cause and effect in an experiment. Although these variables are in a sense conflicting and competing, the correct term is *confounding*.

87. **D** Research Methods: Experimental, Correlational, and Clinical Research
In a double-blind experiment, neither the participants nor the researchers know which group the participants belong to. The purpose of this procedure is to remove the effects of expectation as a confounding variable. If participants expect to be affected by a treatment, they may feel they've been affected only because they expected or wanted to be affected. Similarly, if researchers expect the participants to be affected by a treatment, they may inadvertently influence the participants' perception that they have indeed been affected. The double-blind procedure helps minimize the effects of expectation and ensure that any effects have been caused by the treatment itself.

88. **C** Testing and Individual Differences: Types of Tests
Most classroom tests and exams are achievement tests, which measure what someone has learned. The two closest answer choices—intelligence tests and aptitude tests—differ from achievement tests significantly. Intelligence tests measure mental abilities, not learned material. Aptitude tests are meant to predict future performance, such as in college or in a job, rather than previously learned material.

89. **D** Motivation and Emotion: Social Motives
Incentives are external forces that influence behavior by increasing or decreasing internal drives. Incentives may be positive or negative rewards or punishments, such as money, respect from peers, or the risk of ruining one's reputation. Instinct, drive, and hunger describe intrinsic, not extrinsic, forces, and motivation is the general term that encompasses the idea of behaving in general.

90. **E** Cognition: Problem Solving and Creativity
A heuristic is a "rule-of-thumb" procedure. As a rule of thumb, milk is shelved with other dairy products in the dairy section. Joey's decision to take a heuristic approach to solving this problem does not *guarantee* he will find his milk, but it should be quicker than the more methodical algorithmic approach, which would require him to search every aisle of the store. Concept and prototype generally do not apply to problem solving, and insight is not a strategic problem-solving method.

91. **D**   Personality: Self-concept, Self-esteem

The importance of self-esteem is most often associated with the humanistic perspective, which emphasizes the growth potential of healthy people. Humanistic psychologists study personality in hopes of fostering personal growth.

92. **C**   History and Approaches: Approaches/Cognitive

The cognitive approach emphasizes what goes on in people's heads, particularly how people reason, remember, understand language, and solve problems. It differs from behaviorism in that it infers mental processes from observable behavior.

93. **C**   Abnormal Psychology: Theories of Psychopathology

The medical model views mental illnesses as illnesses that can be diagnosed from their symptoms and cured by using therapy. The client-centered approach to therapy is a part of the humanistic view of psychology. The biopsychosocial and psychodynamic models are linked to therapeutic perspectives as well. None of these have symptoms and diagnoses as their core, as the medical model does.

94. **A**   Learning: Operant Conditioning

Shaping is an operant conditioning procedure in which the learner is guided toward the final response via reinforcement. Reinforcement comes as the learner achieves successive approximations of the final desired response. In this example, Susan is reinforcing the behavior but also requiring the behavior to change each time and move closer to the final, desired outcome.

95. **A**   Cognition: Thinking

Belief persistence occurs when a person clings to initial conceptions even after they have been shown to be false. In the case of this student, belief persistence may limit the respect he gets from teachers because they continue to expect the worst from him, even though he has been performing well. Belief bias isn't correct because it deals more with beliefs interfering with the reasoning process. Confirmation bias is wrong because it occurs when a person seeks evidence that supports preexisting beliefs (which isn't applicable here, since the student's good performance in school won't confirm the idea that he's a troublemaker).

96. **A**   Treatment of Psychological Disorders: Treatment Approaches/Cognitive Approaches

Electroconvulsive therapy (ECT) is still used today in the treatment of severe depression. In the past it was used most often to treat schizophrenia. Today patients are given both muscle relaxers and general anesthesia when treated with ECT.

97, 98, 99. **E, D, E** Research Methods: Statistics

In statistics, the three major measures of central tendency are the mode, mean, and median. The mode is the score that occurs most often. In #97, a score of 73 occurs more often than any other score. The mean is the average score. In #98, if we add the five scores together and then divide by five, the mean score is 82. The median is the middle score. In #99, if we put the scores in order from highest to lowest, the score in the middle of the list is 80.

100. **B**   History and Approaches: Approaches/Biological
The biological approach to psychology focuses on how bodily events affect behavior, feelings, and thoughts. In this question, the relationship between stress, which is a physical event, and psychological disorders would be of interest to biological psychologists. Biological psychologists also investigate how these physical events interact with events in the external environment to produce perceptions, memories, and behavior.

SECTION II: FREE-RESPONSE EXPLANATIONS

Question 1

Sample Response

The process of perception is the interpretation of the stimuli that we encounter in the world around us. These stimuli are processed in two ways: bottom-up processing, which focuses on the raw stimuli that enters the mind via sensory organs, and top-down processing, which focuses on the effects of experiences and expectations on the interpretation of the incoming stimuli. Several different concepts play important roles in and highlight important ideas about the process of perception.

Gestalt psychology focuses on the concept that the whole is more important than the sum of its parts. Gestalt research would focus on the combination and interaction of all of the stimuli that we encounter and the impact of these stimuli on our perceptions. A variety of visual illusions are excellent examples of Gestalt psychology.

Perceptual set is a predisposition based on our experiences that leads us to perceive stimuli in one way and not in another way. Perceptual set is influenced by cultural and other subjective factors. A schema, which is a mental concept of how things are or should be, is one example of something that influences perceptual set. Perceptual sets can and do change over time through the processes of assimilation and accommodation.

Motion perception is a complicated process that involves the interpretation of a number of factors through perception. These factors include our vestibular and kinesthetic senses, as well as the movement of objects and backgrounds in the world around us. Examples of motion perception include the phi phenomenon, which is responsible for the illusion of movement we experience when observing lights blinking on and off in a preset pattern. Another example of motion perception is the stroboscopic effect, which is the phenomenon that allows our perception of animation and motion pictures.

Depth perception is the ability to see the world in three dimensions and judge distance. Depth perception occurs for a variety of reasons. One of these reasons is monocular cues, such as relative size, relative motion, interposition, relative height, texture gradient, relative clarity, or linear perspective. Relative size is the concept that if we know the size of an object, then if it is small, it must be far away, and if it is large, it must be close by. Relative motion tells us that a known object moving slowly must be far away from us. Interposition relates to the overlap of multiple objects. Relative height tells us that objects that are high in our field of vision must be farther away. Texture gradient informs us that the texture of objects farther away will often be smoother than objects closer to us. Relative clarity is the idea that fuzzy cloudy objects must be farther away. And finally, the linear perspective tells us that parallel lines appear to join together in an upside-down V shape farther away.

Another component of depth perception is binocular cues. These are cues that depend on both eyes. Binocular cues include retinal disparity, which is the slight difference in the images we see on each retina, and convergence, which is the cue that relates to the muscle tension in our eyes as they turn inward slightly to view objects that are close to us.

Context is the setting in which we receive sensory stimuli. This setting causes us to interpret our surroundings based on what we have just experienced. An example of context is the additional stimuli that could interfere with our interpretation and perceptions of objects, distance, color, or location.

Commentary on Question 1

Possible points: 10

- 1 point for each correct definition/explanation of a concept
- 1 point for each appropriate example

When completing this answer, the student should show evidence of a high degree of psychological knowledge concerning the process of perception. In order for a student to receive full credit for each point of this essay, responses must be complete and in depth. The response should also include a specific example of each concept. Neither the explanations nor the examples should be generalities that could be learned from popular literature.

Question 2

Sample Response

Psychological disorders needed to be diagnosed based on symptoms. In order to diagnose a disorder, a psychologist or psychiatrist should refer to the Diagnostic and Statistical Manual of Mental Disorders IV (DSM-IV). *In order to be considered a true psychological disorder, the disorder must be maladaptive, unjustifiable, disturbing, and atypical. There are many types of psychological disorders, each with its own group of typical symptoms.*

Anxiety disorders are disorders associated with apprehension and uneasiness. Many people experience normal anxiety, and not all of these people have anxiety disorders. For it to be a disorder, the anxiety must be persistent and cause distress. Some examples of anxiety disorders include generalized anxiety disorder, panic disorders, phobic disorders, obsessive-compulsive disorders, and post-traumatic stress disorder.

Mood disorders are disturbances of emotions that differ from normal emotions in degree. Symptoms can include lethargy, hopelessness, manic excitement, or swings between manic and depressive states. Two examples of mood disorders are major depressive disorder and bipolar disorder.

Dissociative disorders are characterized by a separation of a person's sense of self from reality and from his or her memories, thoughts, or feelings. A person with a dissociative disorder may experience memory loss or a change in identity. Some examples of dissociative disorders include dissociative amnesia, dissociative fugue, and dissociative identity disorder.

Schizophrenic disorders typically involve disorganized and delusional thinking, disturbed perceptions, and inappropriate emotions and behaviors. People suffering from a schizophrenic disorder may be plagued by false beliefs or by paranoid delusions, and their ability to make sense of the world through selective attention may be severely impaired. Some examples of schizophrenic disorders include paranoid schizophrenia, catatonic schizophrenia, disorganized schizophrenia, and undifferentiated schizophrenia.

Personality disorders are lasting, rigid patterns of behavior that can seriously impair social functioning. A person with a personality disorder may engage in dramatic or eccentric behavior, withdraw from or avoid other people, or display a total lack of conscience. Some examples of personality disorders include narcissistic personality disorder, borderline personality disorder, and antisocial personality disorder.

Commentary on Question 2

Possible points: 10

- 1 point for each correct definition of a concept
- 1 point for correctly identified symptoms of each

When completing this answer, the student should show evidence of a high degree of psychological knowledge concerning psychological disorders and the *DSM-IV*. In order for a student to receive full credit for each point of this essay, responses must be complete and in depth. The response should also include a specific example of each concept. These examples should not be generalities that could be learned from popular literature. Rather, each explanation and example should demonstrate the student's thorough, specific knowledge of the subject.

PRACTICE EXAM 2

AP PSYCHOLOGY PRACTICE EXAM 2 ANSWER SHEET

1. Ⓐ Ⓑ Ⓒ Ⓓ Ⓔ	26. Ⓐ Ⓑ Ⓒ Ⓓ Ⓔ	51. Ⓐ Ⓑ Ⓒ Ⓓ Ⓔ	76. Ⓐ Ⓑ Ⓒ Ⓓ Ⓔ
2. Ⓐ Ⓑ Ⓒ Ⓓ Ⓔ	27. Ⓐ Ⓑ Ⓒ Ⓓ Ⓔ	52. Ⓐ Ⓑ Ⓒ Ⓓ Ⓔ	77. Ⓐ Ⓑ Ⓒ Ⓓ Ⓔ
3. Ⓐ Ⓑ Ⓒ Ⓓ Ⓔ	28. Ⓐ Ⓑ Ⓒ Ⓓ Ⓔ	53. Ⓐ Ⓑ Ⓒ Ⓓ Ⓔ	78. Ⓐ Ⓑ Ⓒ Ⓓ Ⓔ
4. Ⓐ Ⓑ Ⓒ Ⓓ Ⓔ	29. Ⓐ Ⓑ Ⓒ Ⓓ Ⓔ	54. Ⓐ Ⓑ Ⓒ Ⓓ Ⓔ	79. Ⓐ Ⓑ Ⓒ Ⓓ Ⓔ
5. Ⓐ Ⓑ Ⓒ Ⓓ Ⓔ	30. Ⓐ Ⓑ Ⓒ Ⓓ Ⓔ	55. Ⓐ Ⓑ Ⓒ Ⓓ Ⓔ	80. Ⓐ Ⓑ Ⓒ Ⓓ Ⓔ
6. Ⓐ Ⓑ Ⓒ Ⓓ Ⓔ	31. Ⓐ Ⓑ Ⓒ Ⓓ Ⓔ	56. Ⓐ Ⓑ Ⓒ Ⓓ Ⓔ	81. Ⓐ Ⓑ Ⓒ Ⓓ Ⓔ
7. Ⓐ Ⓑ Ⓒ Ⓓ Ⓔ	32. Ⓐ Ⓑ Ⓒ Ⓓ Ⓔ	57. Ⓐ Ⓑ Ⓒ Ⓓ Ⓔ	82. Ⓐ Ⓑ Ⓒ Ⓓ Ⓔ
8. Ⓐ Ⓑ Ⓒ Ⓓ Ⓔ	33. Ⓐ Ⓑ Ⓒ Ⓓ Ⓔ	58. Ⓐ Ⓑ Ⓒ Ⓓ Ⓔ	83. Ⓐ Ⓑ Ⓒ Ⓓ Ⓔ
9. Ⓐ Ⓑ Ⓒ Ⓓ Ⓔ	34. Ⓐ Ⓑ Ⓒ Ⓓ Ⓔ	59. Ⓐ Ⓑ Ⓒ Ⓓ Ⓔ	84. Ⓐ Ⓑ Ⓒ Ⓓ Ⓔ
10. Ⓐ Ⓑ Ⓒ Ⓓ Ⓔ	35. Ⓐ Ⓑ Ⓒ Ⓓ Ⓔ	60. Ⓐ Ⓑ Ⓒ Ⓓ Ⓔ	85. Ⓐ Ⓑ Ⓒ Ⓓ Ⓔ
11. Ⓐ Ⓑ Ⓒ Ⓓ Ⓔ	36. Ⓐ Ⓑ Ⓒ Ⓓ Ⓔ	61. Ⓐ Ⓑ Ⓒ Ⓓ Ⓔ	86. Ⓐ Ⓑ Ⓒ Ⓓ Ⓔ
12. Ⓐ Ⓑ Ⓒ Ⓓ Ⓔ	37. Ⓐ Ⓑ Ⓒ Ⓓ Ⓔ	62. Ⓐ Ⓑ Ⓒ Ⓓ Ⓔ	87. Ⓐ Ⓑ Ⓒ Ⓓ Ⓔ
13. Ⓐ Ⓑ Ⓒ Ⓓ Ⓔ	38. Ⓐ Ⓑ Ⓒ Ⓓ Ⓔ	63. Ⓐ Ⓑ Ⓒ Ⓓ Ⓔ	88. Ⓐ Ⓑ Ⓒ Ⓓ Ⓔ
14. Ⓐ Ⓑ Ⓒ Ⓓ Ⓔ	39. Ⓐ Ⓑ Ⓒ Ⓓ Ⓔ	64. Ⓐ Ⓑ Ⓒ Ⓓ Ⓔ	89. Ⓐ Ⓑ Ⓒ Ⓓ Ⓔ
15. Ⓐ Ⓑ Ⓒ Ⓓ Ⓔ	40. Ⓐ Ⓑ Ⓒ Ⓓ Ⓔ	65. Ⓐ Ⓑ Ⓒ Ⓓ Ⓔ	90. Ⓐ Ⓑ Ⓒ Ⓓ Ⓔ
16. Ⓐ Ⓑ Ⓒ Ⓓ Ⓔ	41. Ⓐ Ⓑ Ⓒ Ⓓ Ⓔ	66. Ⓐ Ⓑ Ⓒ Ⓓ Ⓔ	91. Ⓐ Ⓑ Ⓒ Ⓓ Ⓔ
17. Ⓐ Ⓑ Ⓒ Ⓓ Ⓔ	42. Ⓐ Ⓑ Ⓒ Ⓓ Ⓔ	67. Ⓐ Ⓑ Ⓒ Ⓓ Ⓔ	92. Ⓐ Ⓑ Ⓒ Ⓓ Ⓔ
18. Ⓐ Ⓑ Ⓒ Ⓓ Ⓔ	43. Ⓐ Ⓑ Ⓒ Ⓓ Ⓔ	68. Ⓐ Ⓑ Ⓒ Ⓓ Ⓔ	93. Ⓐ Ⓑ Ⓒ Ⓓ Ⓔ
19. Ⓐ Ⓑ Ⓒ Ⓓ Ⓔ	44. Ⓐ Ⓑ Ⓒ Ⓓ Ⓔ	69. Ⓐ Ⓑ Ⓒ Ⓓ Ⓔ	94. Ⓐ Ⓑ Ⓒ Ⓓ Ⓔ
20. Ⓐ Ⓑ Ⓒ Ⓓ Ⓔ	45. Ⓐ Ⓑ Ⓒ Ⓓ Ⓔ	70. Ⓐ Ⓑ Ⓒ Ⓓ Ⓔ	95. Ⓐ Ⓑ Ⓒ Ⓓ Ⓔ
21. Ⓐ Ⓑ Ⓒ Ⓓ Ⓔ	46. Ⓐ Ⓑ Ⓒ Ⓓ Ⓔ	71. Ⓐ Ⓑ Ⓒ Ⓓ Ⓔ	96. Ⓐ Ⓑ Ⓒ Ⓓ Ⓔ
22. Ⓐ Ⓑ Ⓒ Ⓓ Ⓔ	47. Ⓐ Ⓑ Ⓒ Ⓓ Ⓔ	72. Ⓐ Ⓑ Ⓒ Ⓓ Ⓔ	97. Ⓐ Ⓑ Ⓒ Ⓓ Ⓔ
23. Ⓐ Ⓑ Ⓒ Ⓓ Ⓔ	48. Ⓐ Ⓑ Ⓒ Ⓓ Ⓔ	73. Ⓐ Ⓑ Ⓒ Ⓓ Ⓔ	98. Ⓐ Ⓑ Ⓒ Ⓓ Ⓔ
24. Ⓐ Ⓑ Ⓒ Ⓓ Ⓔ	49. Ⓐ Ⓑ Ⓒ Ⓓ Ⓔ	74. Ⓐ Ⓑ Ⓒ Ⓓ Ⓔ	99. Ⓐ Ⓑ Ⓒ Ⓓ Ⓔ
25. Ⓐ Ⓑ Ⓒ Ⓓ Ⓔ	50. Ⓐ Ⓑ Ⓒ Ⓓ Ⓔ	75. Ⓐ Ⓑ Ⓒ Ⓓ Ⓔ	100. Ⓐ Ⓑ Ⓒ Ⓓ Ⓔ

AP PSYCHOLOGY
SECTION I
Time—1 hour and 10 minutes
100 Questions

<u>Directions:</u> Each of the questions or incomplete statements below is followed by five suggested answers or completions. Select the one that is best in each case and then fill in the corresponding oval on the answer sheet.

1. In psychology, "behavior" is best defined as

   (A) anything a person sees, does, or feels
   (B) any action an observer perceives as important
   (C) any action, whether observable or not
   (D) anything we can infer from a person's actions
   (E) any action we can observe and record

2. Basic needs often motivate human behavior. In order to meet higher-order needs, one must first meet those basic needs, an idea referred to as a hierarchy of needs. Who conceptualized this theory?

   (A) Maslow
   (B) Cannon
   (C) Skinner
   (D) Pavlov
   (E) Kinsey

3. One of the most feared brain ailments of old age involves the deterioration of neurons that produce acetylcholine, a condition called

   (A) dementia
   (B) savant syndrome
   (C) Alzheimer's
   (D) stroke
   (E) aneurysm

4. All of the following correctly describe the process of the action potential EXCEPT

   (A) the neuron fires an impulse when it receives signals from sense receptors
   (B) during the refractory period, the neuron pumps positively charged ions back outside the axon
   (C) when the action potential reaches an axon terminal, it stimulates the release of neurotransmitters
   (D) electrical impulses travel from one neuron to another across the cerebral gap
   (E) the fluid-filled interior of a resting axon is full of negatively charged ions

5. Some people are motivated to accomplish tasks such as mountain climbing, parachuting, or running a marathon. Which theory of motivation best explains this behavior?

   (A) Arousal theory
   (B) Cannon-Bard theory
   (C) Instinct theory
   (D) Drive-reduction theory
   (E) James-Lange theory

6. The type of psychological research most vulnerable to the effects of wording is

   (A) naturalistic observation
   (B) case study
   (C) correlation
   (D) statistical significance
   (E) survey

7. Twins that are genetically identical are known as

   (A) fraternal twins
   (B) dizygotic twins
   (C) maternal twins
   (D) monozygotic twins
   (E) both C and D

8. Lilly is concerned for the health of her unborn child because she was exposed to possibly dangerous chemicals at work. What specifically is she concerned about?

   (A) Imprinting
   (B) Reuptake
   (C) Teratogens
   (D) Dermatogens
   (E) Lesions

9. Damage to what brain structure can result in either extreme, insatiable hunger or a total lack of interest in food?

   (A) Hypothalamus
   (B) Hippocampus
   (C) Angular gyrus
   (D) Prefrontal cortex
   (E) Pons

GO ON TO THE NEXT PAGE

AP PSYCHOLOGY MULTIPLE-CHOICE QUESTIONS

10. What subtype of schizophrenia often involves a preoccupation with delusions or hallucinations?

    (A) Paranoid
    (B) Disorganized
    (C) Catatonic
    (D) Undifferentiated
    (E) Residual

11. What structure provides internal communication for sensory and motor inputs in the central nervous system?

    (A) Cell body
    (B) Interneuron
    (C) Dendrite
    (D) Synaptic cleft
    (E) Pituitary gland

12. Which of the following is best associated with the concept of basic trust formation in children?

    (A) Piaget
    (B) Erikson
    (C) Bandura
    (D) Kohlberg
    (E) Skinner

13. Who was the author of a controversial study from the 1950s concerning American sexual behavior?

    (A) Kinsey
    (B) Skinner
    (C) Freud
    (D) Watson
    (E) Bandura

14. The overabundance of what substance in the brain is often linked to schizophrenia?

    (A) Dopamine
    (B) Serotonin
    (C) Mercury
    (D) Endorphins
    (E) Acetylcholine

15. Jim has been labeled a poor student by his teachers, who hesitated to call his parents for fear of being proved wrong. Jim's parents said they might believe the teachers if Jim continued to perform poorly on exams. Although Jim does well on exams about half the time, his teachers report that he is still performing badly. Their tendency to remember his poor scores instead of his good scores is called

    (A) belief persistence
    (B) belief bias
    (C) overconfidence
    (D) generalization
    (E) confirmation bias

16. Douglas has been diagnosed with borderline personality disorder. Which of these best describes his behavior?

    (A) He displays a rigid, maladaptive personality pattern that causes him not to get along with others
    (B) He has intense but unstable relationships and fears abandonment
    (C) He lies, steals, manipulates others, and shows a lack of guilt
    (D) He has an exaggerated sense of self-importance and self-absorption
    (E) He displays delusional behavior associated with hallucinations

17. Which of the following statements is NOT true about achievement motivation?

    (A) Achievement is almost exclusively determined by extrinsic forces
    (B) According to Maslow, basic needs must first be meet in order to aspire to higher goals
    (C) High achievers often spend more time in practice and rehearsal than low achievers
    (D) High achievement has both emotional and cognitive roots
    (E) People with a high need for achievement tend to be more persistent

18. The concept of cognitive development consisting of four distinct stages is credited to

    (A) Piaget
    (B) Erikson
    (C) Bandura
    (D) Kohlberg
    (E) Skinner

GO ON TO THE NEXT PAGE

19. Some patients who suffer from severe epilepsy have not responded to other treatments, but they have found relief through a radical surgery in which the doctor surgically cuts the

    (A) hippocampus
    (B) corpus callosum
    (C) medulla
    (D) motor cortex
    (E) amygdala

20. Wilma disappears without a trace for several months after experiencing extreme stress. One year later, she is found living in another state with a new identity. When questioned by the police, Wilma had no memory beyond one previous year. No physical or drug explanation exists for this memory loss. What condition does Wilma seem to have?

    (A) Seasonal affective disorder
    (B) Dissociative identity disorder
    (C) Dissociative fugue
    (D) Narcissistic personality disorder
    (E) Bipolar disorder

21. Which of the following theories of emotion states that an emotionally arousing experience causes simultaneous triggering of a physiological reaction and the subjective experience of emotion?

    (A) Cannon-Bard theory
    (B) James-Lange theory
    (C) Two-factor theory
    (D) Opponent-process theory
    (E) Drive-reduction theory

22. Which of the following lists of gestational stages is in the correct order?

    (A) Zygote-embryo-fetus
    (B) Embryo-zygote-fetus
    (C) Fetus-embryo-zygote
    (D) Zygote-fetus-embryo
    (E) Fetus-zygote-embryo

23. Carl Rogers developed an approach to psychotherapy that involves active listening on the part of the therapist and an empathetic environment. This approach is described as

    (A) client centered
    (B) psychoanalytic
    (C) behavioral
    (D) eclectic
    (E) biological

24. What aspect of a person is responsible for distorting logical reasoning and confusing his or her conclusions, thus leading to belief bias?

    (A) Ego
    (B) Motivation
    (C) Overconfidence
    (D) Belief perseverance
    (E) Preexisting beliefs

25. In an experiment, the hypothesis is

    (A) a statement of the findings
    (B) a statement based on extrinsic facts
    (C) a statement that is proved true
    (D) a statement of the expected results
    (E) rarely postulated prior to obtaining the results

26. Which theory of emotion focuses on high and low arousal and whether an emotion is pleasant or unpleasant?

    (A) Two-dimension theory
    (B) James-Lange
    (C) Two-factor theory
    (D) Opponent-process theory
    (E) Cannon-Bard

27. People often construct a mental image of the best model of a concept or category. This image is called a(n)

    (A) cognition
    (B) concept
    (C) prototype
    (D) heuristic
    (E) insight

28. At which stage of psychosocial development does a person need to exercise will and do things independently?

    (A) Trust vs. mistrust
    (B) Autonomy vs. shame and doubt
    (C) Initiative vs. guilt
    (D) Identity vs. role confusion
    (E) Intimacy vs. isolation

GO ON TO THE NEXT PAGE

AP PSYCHOLOGY MULTIPLE-CHOICE QUESTIONS

29. Why do neurons in the brain often cluster together to form neural networks?

    (A) To better provide simple automatic responses to sensory stimuli
    (B) To release endorphins
    (C) To strengthen connections that produce a given output in response to a given pattern of inputs
    (D) To produce lesions on the brain
    (E) To allow the limbic system to regulate the prefrontal cortex

30. Bill is in a psychoanalytic therapy session. The therapist asks him to discuss whatever comes to his mind about an event in his childhood. Bill is hesitant to discuss the event because he is embarrassed. Which of these terms would his therapist use to describe why Bill was hesitant to discuss the event?

    (A) Transference
    (B) Resistance
    (C) Systematic desensitization
    (D) Generalization
    (E) Assimilation

31. Which part of the nervous system regulates the fight-or-flight instinct?

    (A) Sympathetic nervous system
    (B) Somatic nervous system
    (C) Autonomic nervous system
    (D) Parasympathetic nervous system
    (E) Peripheral nervous system

32. After hearing a news story about a recent airline crash, Bobbie is afraid to fly. Her husband attempts to talk her into flying by pointing out that statistically, people are much safer on an airplane than in a car. She still refuses to fly. Bobbie has calculated her risk using what?

    (A) Availability heuristic
    (B) Prototyping
    (C) Serial position effect
    (D) Representative heuristic
    (E) An algorithm

33. Sonny is seeking treatment for alcoholism. He goes to a therapist who suggests putting a colorless, odorless substance in the alcohol he drinks that will induce nausea and vomiting. Which of the following techniques is the therapist using?

    (A) Systematic desensitization
    (B) Resistance
    (C) Assimilation
    (D) Generalization
    (E) Aversive conditioning

34. At which stage of psychosocial development does a person work to form close relationships or feel socially isolated?

    (A) Integrity vs. despair
    (B) Autonomy vs. shame and doubt
    (C) Initiative vs. guilt
    (D) Identity vs. role confusion
    (E) Intimacy vs. isolation

35. Weber's law of the difference threshold states which of the following?

    (A) For a person to perceive a difference, two stimuli must differ by a constant minimum percentage
    (B) For a person to perceive a difference, two stimuli must differ by a constant amount, which is the same no matter what the stimuli are
    (C) The just noticeable difference must be lower than the absolute threshold
    (D) Subliminal messages work best on people who have a heightened difference threshold
    (E) Transduction must precede signal detection

36. Bobby takes a college admissions test several times, and all of his scores are nearly identical. What does this suggest about the test he has taken?

    (A) It must be very easy
    (B) It appears to have test-retest reliability
    (C) It must be very hard
    (D) The test needs to be renormed
    (E) The test is out-of-date

GO ON TO THE NEXT PAGE

37. In order to better treat her clients, Molly decides to combine therapies that involve changing self-defeating thinking and changing inappropriate behaviors. This combination would be a form of

(A) cognitive-behavior therapy
(B) psychoanalysis
(C) humanistic therapy
(D) insight therapy
(E) client-centered therapy

38. Warren has been diagnosed with aphasia. An MRI scan of his brain would likely show damage to what region of his brain?

(A) Broca's area
(B) Pons
(C) Prefrontal cortex
(D) Cerebellum
(E) Hypothalamus

39. Marcy first pours liquid into a tall, skinny cup. She then pours the same volume of liquid into a wide, short cup. When Marcy asks a young child which cup has more liquid, the child is unable to see that the volume of the liquid has remained the same even though the shape of the cup changed. This child is in the preoperational stage and has not yet mastered the concept of

(A) egocentrism
(B) object permanence
(C) conservation of matter
(D) generalization
(E) maturation

40. The tragic case of Phineas Gage demonstrates the role of what part of the brain in personality?

(A) Occipital lobe
(B) Medulla
(C) Prefrontal cortex
(D) Cerebellum
(E) Hippocampus

41. One obsolete form of psychosurgery involved drilling two holes in the skull and inserting specially designed rods to crush or destroy nerves running from the prefrontal lobes to the rest of the brain in order to reduce the patient's emotional symptoms. This controversial treatment, which is no longer used, is called

(A) electroconvulsive therapy
(B) lobotomy
(C) cingulotomy
(D) transcranial magnetic stimulation
(E) rational emotive behavior therapy

42. U.S. presidents often turn to their cabinet for advice. If the president has voiced support for the issue at hand, the advisers often fail to voice criticisms and concerns. Later, when events show that the course of action was unwise, the president might say, "Why did we not foresee the outcome of this?" The term that best describes what happened to the cabinet is

(A) assimilation
(B) groupthink
(C) accommodation
(D) generalization
(E) social facilitation

43. Which of the following is a basic component of language structure?

(A) Morphemes
(B) Phonemes
(C) Grammar
(D) Syntax
(E) All of the above

44. Which of the following is NOT true about the normal sleep cycle?

(A) As the night goes on, people enter stage 4 sleep less and less
(B) REM sleep periods get longer as the night goes on
(C) Sleep spindles normally occur only in stage 2 sleep
(D) Delta waves are only observed in stage 1 sleep
(E) REM sleep is also known as paradoxical sleep

45. Paul is upset after taking an exam because his professor had told him to study chapter five, but the test actually covered chapter six. His complaint concerns what aspect of this exam?

(A) Split-half reliability.
(B) Content validity
(C) Criterion validity
(D) Predictive validity
(E) Test-retest reliability

46. A psychology professor assumes that one of his students is not intelligent because his test scores are very low. Later, he finds out that the student's parents had recently divorced and a grandparent had just died. What might explain the professor's mistaken assumption about the student?

(A) Fundamental attribution error
(B) Groupthink
(C) Deindividuation
(D) Defense mechanisms
(E) Transference

GO ON TO THE NEXT PAGE

AP PSYCHOLOGY MULTIPLE-CHOICE QUESTIONS

47. Which of the following is NOT true about the physical properties of electromagnetic energy?

    (A) Wavelength is the distance between successive wave peaks
    (B) Hue is determined by light frequency
    (C) Longer-wavelength light has a lower frequency
    (D) Intensity of light is determined by the amplitude of the wave
    (E) Frequency is the number of complete waves that can pass a point in a given time

48. Colson is learning to play the piano. He has memorized the notes on the scale by remembering "Every Good Boy Does Fine" and "Good Boys Do Fine Always." This memory trick is called a(n)

    (A) mnemonic device
    (B) encoding device
    (C) rehearsal cue
    (D) implicit organizer
    (E) explicit organizer

49. Which of the following statements about hypnosis is true?

    (A) Hypnosis is the same as sleep
    (B) Hypnotized people cannot be forced to do things against their will
    (C) People who are submissive, gullible, or likely to conform are more likely to be susceptible to hypnotism
    (D) Hypnotized people have no memory of the experience
    (E) Hypnosis increases the accuracy of memories

50. What process best explains the participation of seemingly good-natured soldiers or police officers in the torture of prisoners?

    (A) Transference
    (B) Entrapment
    (C) Situational attribution
    (D) Dispositional attribution
    (E) Self-serving bias

51. The WAIS and the Stanford-Binet are what kind of tests?

    (A) Intelligence
    (B) Aptitude
    (C) Achievement
    (D) Criterion referenced
    (E) Creativity

52. This behavior was once thought to be a form of mental illness, but recent research has shown that under the right circumstances, almost anyone can be guilty of it. It is considered worse than stereotyping. What is this behavior?

    (A) Prejudice
    (B) Dispositional attribution
    (C) Groupthink
    (D) Ethnocentrism
    (E) Generalization

53. What happens to excess neurotransmitters that are released by the vesicles in the sending neuron?

    (A) They are absorbed by the receptor sites on the receiving neuron
    (B) They become agonists that mimic a particular neurotransmitter
    (C) Through a process called reuptake, they are reabsorbed by the sending neuron
    (D) They remain in the synaptic cleft until the next action potential arrives
    (E) The sending neuron never sends excess neurotransmitters

54. Kelly believes that the best way to study is to stay up all night just before a test. Ashley studies one to two hours a day for one week before the same test. Assuming that both Kelly and Ashley have the same level of intelligence and motivation and that they study for the same number of hours for the test, what idea explains why Ashley is likely to score better on the test than Kelly?

    (A) Serial position effect
    (B) Semantic encoding
    (C) Spacing effect
    (D) Chunking effect
    (E) Rehearsal

55. The major active ingredient of marijuana, THC, would be classified as which of the following?

    (A) Stimulant
    (B) Hallucinogen
    (C) Barbiturate
    (D) Depressant
    (E) Opiate

GO ON TO THE NEXT PAGE

56. Patty Hearst experienced this from of brainwashing, which is sometimes called the Stockholm syndrome, when she was kidnapped by the SLA in the 1970s. What is this phenomenon called?

    (A) Transference
    (B) Foot-in-the-door phenomenon
    (C) Self-serving bias
    (D) Bystander effect
    (E) Cognitive dissonance

57. Which of the following correctly traces the path of sound waves when they enter the ear?

    (A) Tympanic membrane–cochlea–ossicles–auditory cortex–auditory nerve
    (B) Cochlea–tympanic membrane–ossicles–auditory nerve–auditory cortex
    (C) Ossicles–tympanic membrane–cochlea–auditory cortex–auditory nerve
    (D) Tympanic membrane–ossicles–cochlea–auditory nerve–auditory cortex
    (E) Tympanic membrane–ossicles–fovea–auditory nerve–auditory cortex

58. Beth scores poorly on a standardized test. Later, she reads in an article that the test was normed many years ago using military recruits. Based on the information given, what might Beth be thinking about the test as a result of this article?

    (A) The test could be biased against women
    (B) The content validity of the test is high
    (C) The reliability of the test is low
    (D) The test is an example of an achievement test
    (E) All are equally likely

59. Kyndall is concerned about her grade in her psychology, since she earned a zero on a required assignment. Assuming her other grades are all As and Bs, which of the following best describes the impact that her zero will have on her class average?

    (A) Her range of scores will be restricted
    (B) Her zero grade might skew her average
    (C) The zero grade will be the mode score
    (D) Her median score and her mean score should be the same
    (E) None of these can be inferred

60. Vic, a normally peaceful person, gets involved in a large fight at a ball game. When questioned by the police, he states that he was just going along with the crowd. Which of these did Vic experience?

    (A) Normative social influence
    (B) Foot-in-the-door phenomenon
    (C) Self-serving bias
    (D) Deindividuation
    (E) Cognitive dissonance

61. Evelyn says that the name she is trying to remember is on the tip of her tongue. This is a clear failure of

    (A) storage
    (B) retrieval
    (C) encoding
    (D) rehearsal
    (E) generalization

62. What field of psychology emphasizes our tendency to integrate pieces of information into meaningful wholes?

    (A) Perceptualism
    (B) Structuralism
    (C) Functionalism
    (D) Integrationism
    (E) Gestalt

63. Which of the following is NOT true about the motor and sensory cortices?

    (A) Both are located in the lower portions of the cerebellum
    (B) Sensitive areas such as the mouth, fingers, and genitals occupy more cortical space
    (C) The motor cortex controls voluntary movements, while the sensory cortex registers and processes body sensations
    (D) The left hemisphere of the cortices controls and receives information from the right side of the body and vice versa
    (E) The motor cortex is located at the front of the parietal lobe

64. The bystander effect is less likely to occur when which of the following is true?

    (A) A person is not in a hurry
    (B) A person is in a small town or rural area
    (C) A person experiences guilt
    (D) A person is in a good mood
    (E) All are true

GO ON TO THE NEXT PAGE

65. The processing of information into the memory system by means of extracting meaning is called

(A) storage
(B) retrieval
(C) encoding
(D) rehearsal
(E) generalization

66. Ben wants to design a study concerning the effects of violent children's television shows on violent behaviors in children. To ensure that differences among participants are evenly distributed between the control and experimental groups, what should Ben should do?

(A) Place the most aggressive children in the experimental group
(B) Place the most aggressive children in the control group
(C) Randomly assign children to both groups
(D) Place the most passive children in the experimental group
(E) Place the most passive children in the control group

67. Kathy has been blind since birth. A new surgical technique is able to restore her sight at age thirty. What type of research suggests that she will not be likely to recognize objects by sight that she knows by touch?

(A) Sensory deprivation
(B) Accommodation
(C) Transduction
(D) Selective attention
(E) Shape consistency

68. A person who scores very low on a general intelligence test but displays an unbelievable capacity to carry out one specific skill, such as computation or drawing, might be said to have

(A) high creativity
(B) Down syndrome
(C) fetal alcohol syndrome
(D) savant syndrome
(E) mental retardation

69. According to Bandura, which of the following would NOT have to be present for observational learning to be successful?

(A) Intention
(B) Attention
(C) Retention
(D) Ability to reproduce the behavior
(E) Motivation

70. Mike's professor has assigned him the endocrine system as a research topic. Which of these structures should he NOT include in his report?

(A) Ovaries
(B) Pineal gland
(C) Thalamus
(D) Parathyroids
(E) Testes

71. Jordan has experienced significant problems keeping a job and maintaining relationships. A therapist tells him she wants to explore his unconscious by having Jordan relax and talk about whatever comes to his mind, no matter how unimportant it might seem. Which of these best describes the therapist's technique?

(A) Interpretation
(B) Free association
(C) Systematic desensitization
(D) Active listening
(E) Cognitive therapy

72. Who was the creator of the concept of social-cognitive theory?

(A) Bandura
(B) Pavlov
(C) Watson
(D) Skinner
(E) Freud

73. A therapist tells Paula that her id is dominating her behavior. Which of these figures is most associated with the concept of the id?

(A) Freud
(B) Erikson
(C) Piaget
(D) Gilligan
(E) Bandura

74. Infants often demonstrate recognition when they are exposed to photos of their mothers, not just to their mothers' sound and smell. Which of these best explains this phenomenon?

(A) Parallel processing
(B) Feature detectors
(C) Perceptual adaptation
(D) Depth perception
(E) Visual capture

GO ON TO THE NEXT PAGE

AP PSYCHOLOGY MULTIPLE-CHOICE QUESTIONS

75. Frank dislikes his job, but he always works hard because he enjoys the prestige and salary associated with his position. What best explains his behavior?

(A) Frank has experienced intrinsic motivation
(B) Frank has been classically conditioned through acquisition
(C) Frank has experienced extrinsic motivation
(D) Frank has experienced a secondary punisher
(E) Frank is being reinforced via a variable-generalization schedule of reinforcement

76. Which of these is NOT a defense mechanism identified by Freud?

(A) Regression.
(B) Reaction formation
(C) Rationalization
(D) Generalization
(E) Sublimation

77. Janice wants to compare automatic functions such as breathing and heart rate in rats, chimpanzees, and humans. Which portion of the brain should she focus her work on?

(A) Frontal lobe
(B) Medulla
(C) Cerebellum
(D) Hippocampus
(E) All of the above

78. Animation and motion pictures would not appear to be moving if what effect was missing?

(A) Perceptual consistency
(B) Stroboscopic movement
(C) Accommodation
(D) Selective attention
(E) Size consistency

79. What perspective of personality focuses on biologically influenced dispositions such as introversion or extroversion?

(A) Psychodynamic
(B) Psychoanalytic
(C) Trait
(D) Humanistic
(E) Social-cognitive

80. Because of road construction, Farley must take a new, unfamiliar route home. Without any obvious reinforcement, she finds her way home. Which of these terms best explains her success?

(A) Observational learning
(B) Social cognitive theory
(C) Latent learning
(D) Extinction
(E) Generalization

81. Karen has agreed to participate in a research study. She is interviewed in great detail, her friends and family are interviewed, and the researcher observes her over the course of several months. This is an example of

(A) a survey
(B) hypothesis testing
(C) correlational research
(D) a case study
(E) clinical experimentation

82. Harold enjoys very active sports, such as mountain climbing and bungee jumping. What idea suggests that his behavior is determined by the interaction of his personality and environmental factors?

(A) Learned helplessness
(B) Personal control
(C) Internal locus of control
(D) Reciprocal determinism
(E) External locus of control

83. All of the following are consistent with the opponent-process theory EXCEPT

(A) opposing retinal processes make possible color vision
(B) Some cells in the retina are stimulated by one color and inhibited by another
(C) Visual impulses are relayed to the visual cortex via the thalamus
(D) The retina contains three different color receptors
(E) Opponent process explains the effects of afterimages

84. Sandy wants to know how a person's perceived job satisfaction is affected by how often he or she receives a paycheck. She studies teachers who are paid a set salary once a month. Which reinforcement schedule applies to this situation?

(A) Continuous
(B) Variable interval
(C) Fixed ratio
(D) Fixed interval
(E) Variable ratio

GO ON TO THE NEXT PAGE

85. What classic projective testing method requires subjects to interpret various inkblots, thereby revealing their inner feelings?

(A) MMPI
(B) TAT
(C) Stanford-Binet
(D) Myers-Briggs
(E) None of the above

86. Professor Cafaro carefully monitors and records the behaviors of children in a physical education class in order to track the development of their physical skills. Professor Cafaro is most clearly engaged in

(A) naturalistic observation
(B) survey research
(C) experimentation
(D) replication research
(E) psychoanalysis

87. What perspective of personality assumes that people process conscious feelings about themselves in light of their experiences and needs?

(A) Psychodynamic
(B) Psychoanalytic
(C) Trait
(D) Humanistic
(E) Social-cognitive

88. An evolutionary psychologist would agree with all of the following statements EXCEPT

(A) anger facilitated the survival of our ancestors' genes
(B) certain basic brain structures, such as the medulla, have roots in our biological past
(C) nurture is more important than nature in terms of shaping human behavior
(D) in general, males prefer attractive physical features in women, and women prefer men with resources and social status
(E) the prevalence of phobias of spiders, snakes, and heights over fears of gunshots and car accidents demonstrates a genetic predisposition

89. Stan is experiencing unexplained tenseness, uneasiness, apprehension, and a sense that his body is in a continual state of arousal. Which of these would be the diagnosis for Stan?

(A) Panic disorder
(B) Phobic disorder
(C) Obsessive-compulsive disorder
(D) Generalized anxiety disorder
(E) Major depressive disorder

90. What figure is most associated with operant conditioning as well as the creator of a device known as an operant box?

(A) Bandura
(B) Pavlov
(C) Watson
(D) Skinner
(E) Freud

91. Arthur served in World War II and was wounded during the invasion of Iwo Jima. Many years later, images of this experience still intrude on him in flashbacks and nightmares, and he is often startled by loud sounds and noises. He refuses to discuss his experiences with anyone. Which of these would be the diagnosis for Arthur?

(A) Post-traumatic stress disorder
(B) Phobic disorder
(C) Obsessive-compulsive disorder
(D) Generalized anxiety disorder
(E) Major depressive disorder

92. An investigator interested in the relationship between time of year and the rate of suicides in a particular area would probably use the technique of

(A) simple observation
(B) experimentation
(C) correlation
(D) case study
(E) ethnography

93. Who is associated with the famous "Little Albert" research of the 1920s?

(A) Skinner
(B) Bandura
(C) Pavlov
(D) Freud
(E) Watson

GO ON TO THE NEXT PAGE

AP PSYCHOLOGY MULTIPLE-CHOICE QUESTIONS

94. Stephanie seems to continually experience a variety of physical symptoms ranging from headaches to vague body and joint pains. Medical examinations fail to reveal any physical cause for these pains. What would be an appropriate diagnosis for Stephanie?

    (A) Post-traumatic stress disorder
    (B) Hypochondriasis
    (C) Obsessive-compulsive disorder
    (D) Generalized anxiety disorder
    (E) Phobic disorder

95. What portion of the brain includes the visual areas, which receive visual information from the opposite visual field?

    (A) Frontal lobe
    (B) Parietal lobe
    (C) Occipital lobe
    (D) Medulla
    (E) Cerebellum

96. Researchers studying rates of clinical depression and suicide notice that the diagnosis rates of these conditions tend to be higher in winter months. Another name for this phenomenon is

    (A) seasonal affective disorder
    (B) dysrhythmia disorder
    (C) hypochondriasis
    (D) narcissistic personality disorder
    (E) amanic episode

97. The single-blind procedure would be most likely to minimize what on the part of the participants?

    (A) Random assignment
    (B) Replication
    (C) Observational definitions
    (D) The placebo effect
    (E) Standard deviations

98. What approach to psychotherapy attributes thoughts and actions to unconscious motives and conflicts?

    (A) Psychoanalytic
    (B) Humanistic
    (C) Behavioral
    (D) Eclectic
    (E) Biological

99. Carla has a fear of snakes. While cleaning her garage, she mistakes a piece of rope for a snake. She screams and flees. What classical-conditioning term describes why she was afraid of the rope?

    (A) Stimulus discrimination
    (B) Generalization
    (C) Spontaneous recovery
    (D) Higher-order conditioning
    (E) Negative reinforcement

100. What subtype of schizophrenia often involves immobility or excessive, purposeless movements?

    (A) Paranoid
    (B) Disorganized
    (C) Catatonic
    (D) Undifferentiated
    (E) Residual

END OF SECTION I

IF YOU FINISH BEFORE TIME IS CALLED, YOU MAY
CHECK YOUR WORK ON THIS SECTION.

DO NOT GO ON TO SECTION II UNTIL YOU ARE TOLD TO DO SO.

AP PSYCHOLOGY
SECTION II

Time—50 minutes
Percent of total grade—33 $\frac{1}{3}$

Section II consists of two questions that each make up half of the score for Section II. You must answer both questions, using about half your time for each question. If you have extra time at the end of the exam, you may work on your responses.

AP PSYCHOLOGY
SECTION II

Time—50 minutes
Percent of total grade—33 $\frac{1}{3}$

<u>Directions:</u> You have 50 minutes to answer BOTH of the following questions. It is not enough to answer a question by merely listing facts. You should present a cogent argument based on your critical analysis of the question posed, using appropriate psychological terminology.

1. Imagine that you are a psychology student in a college introductory psychology class. Design an experiment using the following terms related to classical conditioning. Be sure to identify each term clearly:

    A. unconditioned stimulus
    B. conditioned stimulus
    C. unconditioned response
    D. conditioned response
    E. acquisition
    F. extinction

GO ON TO THE NEXT PAGE

AP PSYCHOLOGY FREE-RESPONSE QUESTIONS

2. Trace a sensory nerve impulse from the dendrite of a neuron to the sensory cortex of the brain and a motor nerve impulse from the motor cortex back to a voluntary muscle in the body. Be sure to identify and describe all of the parts and processes of the neuron and the action potential as well as the components of the nervous system that are involved in this process. The following terms should be identified clearly in your response:

    A. neuron
    B. dendrites
    C. axon
    D. action potential
    E. peripheral nervous system
    F. central nervous system
    G. sensory cortex
    H. motor cortex

END OF EXAMINATION

PRACTICE EXAM 2: ANSWERS & EXPLANATIONS

Answer Key for Practice Exam 2

Number	Answer	Right	Wrong	Number	Answer	Right	Wrong	Number	Answer	Right	Wrong
1	E	___	___	35	A	___	___	68	D	___	___
2	A	___	___	36	B	___	___	69	A	___	___
3	C	___	___	37	A	___	___	70	C	___	___
4	D	___	___	38	A	___	___	71	B	___	___
5	A	___	___	39	C	___	___	72	A	___	___
6	E	___	___	40	C	___	___	73	A	___	___
7	E	___	___	41	B	___	___	74	B	___	___
8	C	___	___	42	B	___	___	75	C	___	___
9	A	___	___	43	E	___	___	76	D	___	___
10	A	___	___	44	D	___	___	77	B	___	___
11	B	___	___	45	B	___	___	78	B	___	___
12	B	___	___	46	A	___	___	79	C	___	___
13	A	___	___	47	B	___	___	80	C	___	___
14	A	___	___	48	A	___	___	81	D	___	___
15	E	___	___	49	B	___	___	82	D	___	___
16	B	___	___	50	B	___	___	83	D	___	___
17	A	___	___	51	A	___	___	84	D	___	___
18	A	___	___	52	A	___	___	85	E	___	___
19	B	___	___	53	C	___	___	86	A	___	___
20	C	___	___	54	C	___	___	87	D	___	___
21	B	___	___	55	B	___	___	88	C	___	___
22	A	___	___	56	B	___	___	89	D	___	___
23	A	___	___	57	D	___	___	90	D	___	___
24	E	___	___	58	A	___	___	91	A	___	___
25	D	___	___	59	B	___	___	92	C	___	___
26	A	___	___	60	D	___	___	93	E	___	___
27	C	___	___	61	B	___	___	94	B	___	___
28	B	___	___	62	E	___	___	95	C	___	___
29	C	___	___	63	A	___	___	96	A	___	___
30	B	___	___	64	E	___	___	97	D	___	___
31	D	___	___	65	C	___	___	98	A	___	___
32	A	___	___	66	C	___	___	99	B	___	___
33	E	___	___	67	A	___	___	100	C	___	___
34	E	___	___								

HOW TO CALCULATE YOUR SCORE

Section I: Multiple Choice

$$\underline{\hspace{2cm}} - (\tfrac{1}{4} \times \underline{\hspace{2cm}}) = \underline{\hspace{2cm}} = \underline{\hspace{3cm}}$$

Number Correct (out of 100) Number Wrong Multiple-Choice Score Weighted Section I Score (Do not round.)

Section II: Free Response

Question 1 $\underline{\hspace{2cm}}$ × 2.5000 = $\underline{\hspace{2cm}}$
(out of 10)

Question 2 $\underline{\hspace{2cm}}$ × 3.1250 = $\underline{\hspace{2cm}}$
(out of 8)

$$\underline{\hspace{2cm}} + \underline{\hspace{2cm}} = \underline{\hspace{2cm}}$$

Question 1 Score   Question 2 Score   Weighted Section II Score (Do not round.)

Composite Score

$$\underline{\hspace{2cm}} + \underline{\hspace{2cm}} = \underline{\hspace{2cm}}$$

Weighted Section I Score   Weighted Section II Score   Composite Score (Round to the nearest whole number.)

Composite Score*	AP Grade	Interpretation
93–150	5	extremely well qualified
72–92	4	well qualified
53–71	3	qualified
34–52	2	possibly qualified
0–33	1	no recommendation

*Each year the Development Committee determines the formulas used to calculate the raw composite scores. The Chief Faculty Consultant determines how the composite scores fit into the 5-point AP scale.

SECTION I: MULTIPLE-CHOICE EXPLANATIONS

1.   **E**   History and Approaches: Approaches/Behavioral
Behaviorists define "behavior" as observable and measurable acts and events that take place in the environment. Behaviorists focus on environmental rewards and punishers that maintain or discourage behavior. They do not generally invoke the mind or mental states to explain behavior.

2.   **A**   Motivation and Emotion: Biological Bases
Maslow's research indicated that some needs, such as food, water, and shelter, take priority over other needs, such as self-esteem and self-actualization. He called this a hierarchy of needs.

3.   **C**   Developmental Psychology: Life-Span Approach
Alzheimer's is a disease related to declines in the production of acetylcholine. Neurons that produce acetylcholine show shriveled proton filaments and plaques built up on the tips of the neuron branches.

4.   **D**   Biological Bases of Behavior: Functional Organization of the Nervous System
Neurons, or nerve cells, are the basic building blocks of our nervous system. These specialized cells consist of a central cell body surrounded by dendrites, which receive neural stimulation. This information is then passed up the axon to other neurons, muscles, or glands. The neuron fires an electrical impulse when stimulated, which is known as the action potential. As this electrical impulse travels up the axon, it produces a change in electrical charge known as *depolarization*. In order for depolarization to occur, the action potential must reach the threshold, which is the level of neural stimulation needed to trigger a neural impulse.

5.   **A**   Motivation and Emotion: Theories of Motivation
Some behaviors are not motivated by physiological needs such as hunger. These behaviors seem motivated by a need or desire to increase arousal and stimulation. Arousal theory attempts to explain these types of behaviors.

6.   **E**   Research Methods: Experimental, Correlational, and Clinical Research
The survey method, used in many types of psychological research, asks people to report their behavior or opinions. This is a self-report method. Since people's perceptions of their own behavior and opinions can be skewed, the wording of the questions asked on the survey can have a significant effect on the outcome. Even subtle changes in the order or wording of questions can have major effects on the results.

7.   **E**   Biological Bases of Behavior: Genetics
Identical twins are also known as maternal or monozygotic twins. They share genetic information and develop when a fertilized egg divides into two parts and develops into two separate embryos. Nonidentical twins are referred to as fraternal or dizygotic. They develop from two separate eggs fertilized by two separate sperm cells and are no more alike genetically than any other siblings.

8.   **C**   Developmental Psychology: Heredity-Environment Issues

Teratogens are agents that are able to cross the placental barrier from the mother to an unborn child. Some can be environmental; others can be substances the mother ingests, such as alcohol, drugs, or cigarette smoke.

9.   **A**   Motivation and Emotion: Hunger, Thirst, Sex, and Pain

The hypothalamus is the brain's hunger regulator. Stimulation of certain areas of the hypothalamus can bring on extreme hunger, while damage to some areas can create a total lack of interest in food. The other structures listed as answer choices do not regulate hunger.

10.   **A**   Abnormal Psychology: Schizophrenic Disorders

Schizophrenia is a psychotic disorder characterized by disorganized and delusional thinking, disturbed perceptions, and inappropriate actions and emotions. Paranoid disorders are characterized by a preoccupation with delusions and hallucinations. The person finds it difficult to distinguish reality from the delusions and hallucinations.

11.   **B**   Biological Bases of Behavior: Functional Organization of the Nervous System

When information is sent to the brain via sensory neurons, that information is processed via a type of neuron known as an interneuron. The interneuron provides internal communication and intervention between sensory and motor neurons.

12.   **B**   Developmental Psychology: Heredity-Environment Issues

Basic trust is the sense that the world is predictable and trustworthy. Erikson's research supports the idea that early parenting by loving and sensitive caregivers forms the basis for lifelong trust.

13.   **A**   Motivation and Emotion: Hunger, Thirst, Sex, and Pain

Alfred Kinsey interviewed approximately 18,000 people about their sexual behavior, and his report, containing surprising statistics about issues such as premarital sex and masturbation, became an instant best seller. However, Kinsey's methodology and findings are suspect since a large number of the people he interviewed were white, educated, and urban.

14.   **A**   Abnormal Psychology: Schizophrenic Disorders

Autopsies of schizophrenic patients often show as much as a sixfold increase in the number of dopamine receptors in the brain. The overabundance of dopamine might well explain the delusions and hallucinations that schizophrenics often experience, since excessive dopamine may lead to overstimulation of the brain.

15.   **E**   Cognition: Thinking

Confirmation bias occurs when a person seeks evidence that supports preexisting beliefs. The teachers believed Jim was a poor student and didn't want to be proved wrong, so they paid more attention to the evidence that supported their beliefs—his poor scores. Belief persistence isn't correct because it occurs when a person clings to initial conceptions even after they have been shown to be false, which Jim hasn't completely done—he still performs badly about half the time. Belief bias isn't correct because it deals more with beliefs interfering with the reasoning process.

16.   **B**   Abnormal Psychology: Personality Disorders

Borderline personality disorder is characterized by periods of having intense but unstable relationships, during which the person often swings between intense attachment and extreme estrangement from the partner. The person often experiences an overwhelming sense of abandonment, even when that abandonment is only imagined.

17. **A**   Motivation and Emotion: Social Motives
Achievement motivation, a desire for significant accomplishment, is shaped by both intrinsic and extrinsic forces. The other answer choices do characterize achievement motivation. Typically, a person's basic needs have to be met in order for that person to achieve, and high achievers tend to spend much more time than the typical person in preparation for a task. Achievement motivation is usually present at a very young age and has both emotional and cognitive roots.

18. **A**   Developmental Psychology: Developmental Theories
Jean Piaget pioneered the investigation of cognitive development in humans from birth to adulthood. He identified four stages of cognitive development: sensorimotor, preoperational, concrete operational, and formal operational.

19. **B**   Biological Bases of Behavior: Physiological Techniques
The corpus callosum is a wide band of axon fibers that connects the two hemispheres of the brain. Researchers discovered that animals and humans who suffered from severe, chronic epileptic seizures benefited from this radical surgery, which involved cutting the corpus callosum. Patients generally became seizure-free and lived normal lives. Later research revealed that the two hemispheres of the brain began to operate independently of each other as a result of this surgery, creating a "split-brain" situation.

20. **C**   Abnormal Psychology: Dissociative Disorders
Dissociative fugue is a bizarre disorder in which a person abandons his or her identity for a new one, losing all memory of the real identity. A fugue state is most often the result of extreme stress that causes a person to divorce himself or herself from a real identity in favor of a new, safer identity.

21. **B**   Motivation and Emotion: Theories of Emotion
Emotions arise from the combination of physiological arousal, expressive behavior, and conscious experience. The James-Lange theory of emotion is unique in that it states that we first experience physiological arousal to a stimulus and then react to that physiological arousal with an emotion. The Cannon-Bard theory says we experience the arousal and the emotion at the same time. The two-factor theory concerns the relationship between emotion and cognition, and opponent-process theory states that every emotion comes with an opposing emotion. The drive-reduction theory concerns motivation, not emotion.

22. **A**   Developmental Psychology: Dimensions of Development/Physical
The zygote stage lasts from conception to two weeks. The embryo stage lasts from two weeks to eight weeks. The fetus stage lasts from nine weeks to birth.

23. **A**   Treatment of Psychological Disorders: Treatment Approaches/Insight
    Therapies: Psychodynamic/Humanistic Approaches
Carl Rogers's client-centered therapy is a humanistic approach that assumes that the client holds the key to self-fulfillment. By using active listening, the therapist can paraphrase, clarify, and reflect the feelings of the client without interpreting or directing the client.

24.   **E**   Cognition: Thinking

Belief bias is the tendency for preexisting beliefs to distort judgment and decision making. Belief bias often occurs when logical thinking goes too far or when incorrect or perhaps prejudicial beliefs prevent a person from making logical decisions. Belief bias differs from belief perseverance in that belief perseverance occurs when a person insists on maintaining his or her beliefs even in the face of contradictory evidence.

25.   **D**   Research Methods: Experimental

The formation of a hypothesis is a crucial part of psychological experimentation since it gives direction and focus to research. A hypothesis is a testable prediction that is often implied in a theory. The correct order of experimentation would be: 1. the postulation of a theory, 2. the development of a testable prediction, the hypothesis, and 3. research and observations to support or refute the hypothesis.

26.   **A**   Motivation and Emotion: Theories of Emotion

Emotions arise from the combination of physiological arousal, expressive behavior, and conscious experience. Two-dimension theory focuses on rating emotions and placing them on a continuum. One dimension of the continuum is high versus low arousal. The other dimension of the continuum is negative valence (unpleasant) versus positive valence (pleasant).

27.   **C**   Cognition: Thinking

When the mind forms categories or concepts of things, it also forms a prototype, which is the mind's best example of something. When new information is integrated into the mind, the mind compares it against various prototypes until it finds the correct concept grouping for the new information.

28.   **B**   Developmental Psychology: Dimensions of Development/Social

Erik Erikson was interested in the social development of individuals. He believed that each stage of life involved some type of crisis that must be resolved in order to move on to the next stage. In this question, exercising will is associated with the autonomy vs. shame and doubt stage of development.

29.   **C**   Biological Bases of Behavior: Functional Organization of the Nervous System

The brain forms neural networks in order to create shorter and faster connections within the brain. This means that the brain modifies itself in response to certain stimuli. These new connections allow the brain to accomplish these learned tasks faster and more efficiently.

30.   **B**   Treatment of Psychological Disorders: Treatment Approaches/Insight
          Therapies: Psychodynamic/Humanistic Approaches

In this question, Bill's therapist is asking him to engage in free association, which is when a client discusses whatever comes to his or her mind about an event or experience. Bill's hesitation here is called *resistance*. Resistance occurs because the client is trying to block anxiety-laden material from his or her mind.

31.   **D**   Motivation and Emotion: Stress

The parasympathetic nervous system regulates the fight-or-fight response. It is part of the autonomic nervous system, which controls glands and the muscles of internal organs. The counterpart of the parasympathetic nervous system is the sympathetic nervous system, which calms the body to conserve energy. The other answer choices listed here concern different parts of the nervous system. The peripheral nervous system joins the central nervous system to the rest of the body. The somatic nervous system, which controls skeletal muscles, is part of the peripheral nervous system.

32.   **A**   Cognition: Problem Solving and Creativity

People often make judgments based on the availability of certain cases or events in memory. Many times this availability occurs because these are vivid cases that stand out in our mind, a phenomenon called an *availability heuristic*. This vividness causes us to assume that the case is more common than it is in reality. Since plane crashes are dramatic events that are hard to forget, Bobbie easily calls them to mind, whereas the many car crashes that take place every day are not as vivid or present in her memory.

33.   **E**   Treatment of Psychological Disorders: Treatment Approaches/Behavioral Approaches

The therapist in this question is hoping to make Sonny averse to alcohol using a process called *aversive conditioning*. Aversive conditioning is a type of counterconditioning, which involves using behavioral techniques to teach us to associate a new response with things that triggered unwanted behaviors in the past. Another type of counterconditioning is systematic desensitization, which is the gradual removal of a fear response by continued exposure to the fear-inducing stimulus.

34.   **E**   Developmental Psychology: Dimensions of Development/Social

Erik Erikson was interested in the social development of individuals. He believed that each stage of life involved some type of crisis that must be resolved in order to move on to the next stage. In this example, forming close relationships is associated with the intimacy vs. isolation stage of development.

35.   **A**   Thresholds: Weber's Law

Ernst Weber's research on the difference threshold revealed that a person experiences a just noticeable difference (jnd) in stimuli when the difference is a constant minimum percentage. The exact proportions vary depending on the stimuli. For example, the intensity for light must be different by 8 percent, and for weight the difference must be 2 percent. Answer **B** is not correct because the percentage changes depending on the stimuli.

36.   **B**   Testing and Individual Differences: Reliability and Validity

A good test must provide consistent scores no matter how many times it is taken. This is known as reliability. To test reliability, researchers often correlate the same person's score on two versions of the test. If the scores are very similar, the test is most likely reliable. This is called test-retest reliability.

37.   **A**   Treatment of Psychological Disorders: Cognitive Approaches

Many therapists combine parts of cognitive and behavioral therapies, forming a cognitive-behavioral therapy. The goals of this therapy are to change self-defeating thinking and change inappropriate behaviors using an integrated approach. The other strategies listed as answer choices do not have these two goals as their core.

38.   **A**   Cognition: Language

Aphasia is an impairment of language that is normally caused by damage to the left hemisphere of the frontal lobe. If the impairment involves muscle movements associated with speech, then the damage is most likely in Broca's area.

39.   **C**   Developmental Psychology: Dimensions of Development/Cognitive

Piaget identified the principle of conservation of matter. Conservation, part of concrete operational reasoning, is the understanding that some abstract properties such as mass and volume can remain the same even when the shape of the object changes. Children in the preoperational stage cannot recognize this principle and are often confused by concepts such as mass and volume.

40.   **C**   Biological Bases of Behavior: Neuroanatomy

Phineas Gage was a mild-mannered railroad worker who in 1848 suffered a traumatic brain injury when an inch-thick, three-and-a-half-foot-long metal rod was driven through his skull. Gage survived, but friends reported that he was no longer the same person. His personality changed. He became foul-mouthed, ill-tempered, and undependable. Modern forensic examination of his skull indicates that most of the trauma was centered in his prefrontal cortex. Research indicates that this region of the brain is critical for social judgment, rational thinking, and the ability to make and set goal.

41.   **B**   Treatment of Psychological Disorders: Treatment Approaches/Cognitive
              Approaches

The barbaric practice of prefrontal lobotomy was developed in the 1930s as a method of calming patients with severe emotional disorders. It was preformed on tens of thousands of patients. As a result of the procedure, patients were often apathetic, withdrawn, and unable to care for themselves.

42.   **B**   Social Psychology: Group Dynamics

Groupthink is a mode of thinking that occurs when the desire for harmony in a decision-making group overrides a realistic appraisal of alternatives. Research into the decision-making process in major historical events demonstrates that groupthink can happen when a leader seems to not want criticism or soaring expectations override caution.

43.   **E**   Cognition: Language

All of these are part of the thousands of spoken languages on earth. Phonemes are the smallest basic sounds of a language. Morphemes are the smallest units that carry meaning. Grammar is the system of rules for a language. Syntax is the rules for the ordering of words in a sentence.

44.   **D**   States of Consciousness: Sleep and Dreaming

Delta waves are characteristic of very deep sleep and are noted only in stage 4 sleep. Typically a person descends from stage 1 to stage 4 sleep in the first hour of sleep. Then the person begins to return to stage 3 and stage 2 sleep. It is at that point that REM sleep occurs. REM periods get longer as the night progresses.

45.   **B**   Testing and Individual Differences: Reliability and Validity

Validity is a measure of how well a test measures what it is supposed to. In this example, Paul is upset over the content validity of the test. Content validity is the extent to which a test measures the material that has been taught in a class. In this case, the content validity is very low since the test covers a different chapter than was expected.

46.   **A**   Social Psychology: Attribution Processes

The fundamental attribution error occurs when a person analyzing another person's behavior underestimates the impact of external factors and overestimates the impact of internal factors. People are more likely to explain their own behavior in terms of external influences and others' behavior in terms of internal behavior.

47. **B** Sensation and Perception: Sensory Mechanisms

Light is measured by two basic characteristics: wavelength and intensity. Wavelength, the distance between successive wave peaks, determines the hue, or the color, of light. Frequency is determined by the wavelength. Higher frequencies equal bluish colors, and lower frequencies equal reddish colors. Intensity, the amount of energy in light waves, is determined by the amplitude, or height, of the wave. Greater amplitude equals brighter colors; smaller amplitude equals duller colors.

48. **A** Cognition: Memory

Mnemonic devices are memory aids that use creative organization or vivid imagery to help with remembering. Research has found that they are effective tools for recalling information from memory.

49. **B** States of Consciousness: Hypnosis

Research shows clearly that hypnotized people cannot be forced to do things against their will. Hypnotized people do not exhibit sleeplike brain-wave patterns. Further, personality traits are not related to susceptibility to hypnosis, and memories do not seem to be enhanced by hypnotism. In fact, hypnotism often produces pseudomemories and errors. Finally, people will remember what happened to them under hypnosis unless told to forget it by the hypnotist.

50. **B** Social Psychology: Interpersonal Perception

Entrapment is a process in which individuals feel compelled to escalate their commitment to something, even though they realize it could be wrong, because of the effort and time they've invested into the course of action. This process helps explain why people continue to gamble even after losing a lot of money.

51. **A** Testing and Individual Differences: Types of Tests

The Wechsler Adult Intelligence Scale (WAIS) and Stanford-Binet are two of the best-known and most widely used intelligence tests. Intelligence tests are attempts to measure mental aptitudes and compare them to those of others using a numerical score once known as the intelligence quotient (IQ).

52. **A** Social Psychology: Conformity, Compliance, Obedience

Prejudice is a strong negative stereotype associated with an unreasonable dislike or hatred of a group. Prejudice seems to be rooted in a combination of psychological, social, cultural, and economic factors. Ethnocentrism is the belief that one's own religion, nationality, or ethnicity is superior to anyone else's, but this differs from prejudice in that it does not have strong negative stereotypes at its core (although it may in fact play a role in prejudice).

53. **C** Biological Bases of Behavior: Neural Transmission

Neurotransmitters are the body's method of communicating between neurons. These chemical messengers are released from the vesicle of the sending neuron and bind with receptor sites on the receiving neuron. These chemical messengers unlock tiny channels in the receiving neuron, which then allow ions to enter and start the process of the action potential. Excess neurotransmitters are reabsorbed into the sending neuron via a process called reuptake.

54.　**C**　Cognition: Memory
Although many people attempt to study by cramming the night before a test, research shows that shorter rehearsals spread over a longer time are more effective.

55.　**B**　States of Consciousness: Psychoactive Drug Effects
Delta-9-tetrahydrocannabinol (THC) is a mildly hallucinogenic compound found in marijuana. Some of marijuana's effects are depressive in nature, but the major effect is hallucinogenic.

56.　**B**　Social Psychology: Attitudes and Attitude Change
The foot-in-the-door phenomenon was first observed in U.S. soldiers who were captured in the Korean War. Without using brutality, their captors made many of the prisoners collaborate with them by first getting them to agree to small tasks. As time went on, the requests became larger and larger until some prisoners opted to remain behind in Korea after the war ended.

57.　**D**　Sensation and Perception: Sensory Mechanisms
Sound waves enter the auditory canal and strike the tympanic membrane (eardrum). The sound waves are then converted to mechanical motion by the movement of the eardrum against the ossicles (hammer, anvil, and stirrup). The motion of the ossicles pushes against a snail-shaped, fluid-filled tube called the cochlea. The movement of the fluid stimulates tiny hair cells that send the stimulation to the auditory nerve, which transmits it to the auditory cortex of the brain.

58.　**A**　Testing and Individual Differences: Ethics and Standards in Testing
Many early tests were normed using predominantly white male university students and members of the military. As a result, many tests had to be abandoned or renormed because they were often biased against women and minorities.

59.　**B**　Research Methods: Statistics
In statistics, three of the major measures of central tendency are the mean, median, and mode. The mean is the average score. The median is the middle score. The mode is the score that occurs most often. The range of scores is the distance from the lowest to the highest score. Kyndall's zero would skew the mean score in this example because the zero score is not typical and it increases the range of the scores. Skewing is a situation where this single extreme score increases the distance between the mean and median scores.

60.　**D**　Social Psychology: Aggression/Antisocial Behavior
When deindividuation occurs, an individual loses self-awareness and self-restraint and becomes responsive to group experience. Deindividuation occurs in many group settings.

61.　**B**　Cognition: Memory
Retrieval is the process of getting things out of memory. A failure of retrieval—forgetting—can happen for many reasons: decay, which is the fading away of memory; interference, which occurs when new or old information blocks the memory of a related piece of information; or repression, which is when access to anxiety-laden information has been blocked. Although storage is related to memory, in this question the problem is with the *retrieving* of information, not the storage of it. Encoding and rehearsal are ways of improving memory, and generalization here is not related to memory.

62. **E** Sensation and Perception: Sensory Adaptation
At the beginning of the twentieth century, a group of German psychologists began to investigate how the mind organizes sensations into perceptions. They used the German word *gestalt*, or "form," to describe their discovery. What they found is that the mind likes sensations to be ordered and organized. So when the mind perceives sensations, the mind organizes these into a whole. In other words, our minds trick us into perceiving patterns that may not be really there. Gestalt theory is often used to explain visual illusions.

63. **A** Biological Bases of Behavior: Neuroanatomy
The motor and sensory cortices are not located in the same place: the motor cortex is located at the rear of the frontal lobe, and the sensory cortex is located at the front of the parietal lobe. The other answer choices are true.

64. **E** Social Psychology: Organizational Behavior
The bystander effect is the tendency for any given bystander to fail to intervene if other bystanders are present. Bystanders will be more likely to help when they are not in a hurry, when they are in rural rather than urban areas, when they feel guilty, and/or when they are in a good mood.

65. **C** Cognition: Memory
Encoding is how we get memories into our brains. It is a process of sorting, labeling, and assigning meaning to memories. Those memories that have the most importance or the most rehearsal should later be the easiest ones to recall. The processing of explicit memories happens in the hippocampus.

66. **C** Research Methods: Experimental, Correlational, and Clinical Research
When designing an experiment of this type, researchers have to be careful in the construction of both their control and experimental groups. They want to determine if the treatment, the violent television viewing, has a measurable effect on the later violent behavior. If children are prescreened and placed into groups ahead of time based on past aggressive or passive behavior, then the results of the study will not determine if the treatment had any effect because the children in each group were not similar. Therefore, the most effective method of assignment to the two groups is by random assignment. This way, any difference between the groups can be attributed to the treatment and not to personality or past behavior.

67. **A** Sensation and Perception: Sensory Adaptation
Sensory deprivation research has found that people who are born with severe cataracts and do not have them corrected until adulthood often have difficulty recognizing objects by sight that they know by touch. However, they are often able to distinguish colors. Small children who have the same corrective surgery seem to have no impairment. This suggests that if parts of the visual cortex related to shape are not stimulate in childhood, then those areas fail to develop.

68. **D** Testing and Individual Differences: Intelligence
Savant syndrome is a rare condition in which an individual shows little mental capacity in most areas of life and often has problems communicating. However, they are gifted with extraordinary mental abilities in one specific area, such as computation, drawing, or memory.

69. **A**   Learning: Social Learning

Bandura's research into observational learning showed that attention, retention, the ability to reproduce the behavior, and motivation are needed for observational learning to occur. Intention is not always present because in some situations a person duplicates a behavior without intending to.

70. **C**   Biological Bases of Behavior: Endocrine System

The endocrine system is a group of organs and glands in the body that produce hormones. Hormones are chemical substances that are secreted by glands in the endocrine system. The purpose of these substances is to regulate the functions of other organs. The hypothalamus, not the thalamus, sends signals to the pituitary gland to regulate the endocrine system.

71. **B**   Personality: Personality Theories and Approaches

Free association is a psychoanalytic technique for exploring the unconscious that was often used by Freud. In free association, a person is asked to relax and talk about whatever comes to his or her mind, no matter how unimportant the topic might seem. Freud discovered this technique while exploring the use of hypnosis in therapy.

72. **A**   Learning: Social Learning

Albert Bandura's classic research into observational learning in the 1960s helped create the concept of social-cognitive theory. Social-cognitive theory investigates how behavior is learned through observation of others.

73. **A**   Personality: Personality Theories and Approaches

Freud saw the unconscious mind as the larger part of personality. The id is associated with the unconscious. The ego is associated with the conscious mind, and the superego is associated with the preconscious mind.

74. **B**   Sensation and Perception: Attention

Feature detectors are nerve cells in the brain that respond to specific features of a stimulus, such as angle, shape, and movement. The visual cortex passes this information on to specific areas in the temporal lobe that enable a person to see faces. fMRI scans allow researchers to note specific types of objects that subjects are viewing based on brain activity.

75. **C**   Learning: Cognitive Processes in Learning

In learning, two main methods of motivation have been identified. One is intrinsic, which is internal or self-motivation. The other is extrinsic, or external motivation. Frank gains no personal satisfaction out of his job, so he is therefore externally motivated by prestige and salary.

76. **D**   Personality: Personality Theories and Approaches

According to Freud, defense mechanisms are strategies people use to control their sexual or aggressive impulses in social groups. All of the answer choices listed here are defense mechanisms except for generalization, which is related to conditioning, not psychoanalytic theory.

77. **B**   Biological Bases of Behavior: Neuroanatomy

The medulla, which is located in the brain-stem portion of the brain, regulates automatic functions such as breathing and heart rate in most animals. The medulla is the part of the brain connected to the spinal cord.

78.   **B**   Sensation and Perception: Perceptual Processes

Early animators and filmmakers discovered the stroboscopic effect. Frames of film shown at twenty-four frames per second create the illusion of movement, when in reality what we are seeing is a fast succession of still pictures. The motion we perceive is in our minds.

79.   **C**   Personality: Personality Theories and Approaches

The trait perspective of personality focuses on biologically influenced dispositions such as introversion or extroversion. In this perspective, descriptions of personality are based on fundamental traits, which are a person's characteristic behaviors or motives.

80.   **C**   Learning: Cognitive Processes in Learning

Latent learning is a type of learning that is not expressed in an immediate response. It occurs with no obvious reinforcement. In this example, Farley has drawn on knowledge and skills of driving she has learned previously and applied them to a new situation to solve a problem.

81.   **D**   Research Methods: Experimental, Correlational, and Clinical Research

In a case study, researchers study one or more individuals in great depth in the hope of revealing universal truths. Because of the limited number of individuals studied, the greatest weakness of the case study method is that the individuals may be atypical—that is, they may not accurately represent the whole of the population being studied. A strength of case studies is the fact that certain unique cases can lend great insight to psychologists, allow for more in-depth understanding, and generate new hypotheses.

82.   **D**   Personality: Personality Theories and Approaches

Reciprocal determinism is the idea that Harold's behavior is shaped by the interaction of his personality and environmental factors. This concept differs from the other answer choices in that it focuses on that interaction.

83.   **D**   Sensation and Perception: Perceptual Processes

The trichromatic color theory, not the opponent-process theory, postulated that color vision existed because the retina contained three different color receptors, one each for red, green, and blue. Opponent-process theory was created to help explain facets of color vision that the trichromatic theory of Young-Helmholtz could not explain. Opponent-process theory helps to explain phenomena such as afterimages.

84.   **D**   Learning: Operant Conditioning

Skinner discovered that once a behavior was learned, the reinforcement of that learning could happen on various learning schedules. In this example, the teachers get the same pay once each month—they are on a fixed-interval schedule of reinforcement. This means their pay is fixed, the same amount each month, and the time is fixed, once a month.

85.   **E**   Personality: Assessment Techniques

The correct answer is the Rorschach inkblot test, which was developed in 1921. This test assumes that what a person sees in inkblots reveals his or her inner feelings. Many questions have been raised about this test's reliability, and today it is most often used as a method of stimulating discussion.

86.   **A**   Research Methods: Experimental, Correlational, and Clinical Research

The primary purpose of naturalistic observation is to observe people or animals in their normal social environment. Psychologists use naturalistic observation wherever people happen to be. The key to observational research is that the researcher must carefully and systematically record all of the behaviors that are observed without interfering with, or in many cases participating in, the behaviors.

87. **D**   Personality: Self-concept, Self-esteem
The humanistic perspective emphasizes the growth potential of healthy people. Humanistic psychologists study personality in hopes of fostering personal growth.

88. **C**   History and Approaches: Approaches/Evolutionary/Sociobiological
Evolutionary psychology has been defined as the study of the evolution of behavior and the mind using principles of natural selection. Natural selection is presumed to have favored genes that predisposed behavior tendencies and information-processing systems that solved adaptive problems faced by our ancestors, thus contributing to the survival and spread of their genes. The concept of nurture in psychology is more closely associated with the learning and social-cultural perspectives. Nature, on the other hand, is related to genetic and biological predispositions.

89. **D**   Abnormal Psychology: Anxiety Disorders
Generalized anxiety disorder manifests itself when a person experiences unexplained tenseness and uneasiness, apprehension, and a sense that his or her body is in a continual state of arousal. Often the person is unable to identify a specific cause for this disorder, which adds to the sense of anxiety.

90. **D**   Learning: Operant Conditioning
B. F. Skinner was the creator of the concept known as operant conditioning. He believed that people are controlled by their environmental influences. He set out to scientifically study this influence using a device he called an operant chamber, or Skinner box. In it he could observe how animals learned to accomplish various tasks in order to receive reinforcement or punishment.

91. **A**   Abnormal Psychology: Anxiety Disorders
Post-traumatic stress disorder is a controversial disorder characterized by haunting memories and nightmares, numbed social withdrawal, jumpiness, and anxiety. It is found in people who witness severely threatening and/or uncontrollable events with a sense of fear, helplessness, and horror. It is very common in combat veterans and survivors of atrocities.

92. **C**   Research Methods: Statistics
The correlation coefficient is a statistical measure of relationship. Correlation helps reveal how closely two things vary together and therefore how well either one predicts the other. A negative correlation indicates that two things have an inverse relationship. In other words, one thing leads to the opposite effect in the other. A positive correlation indicates that one thing increases in direct proportion to an increase in another.

93. **E**   Learning: Classical Conditioning
John B. Watson wanted to demonstrate that fears could be conditioned. Although considered highly unethical today, Watson and his colleagues conditioned an eleven-month-old baby known only as "Little Albert" to fear small furry animals. Later tests revealed that this fear had generalized to other hairy or furry objects.

94. **B** Abnormal Psychology: Somatoform Disorders
Somatoform disorders are psychological disorders that cause medically unexplainable symptoms. These disorders were often dismissed in the past as being fantasies in the mind of the patient. Hypochondriasis is a specific type of somatoform disorder in which patients really do suffer because they are convinced they are actually ill.

95. **C** Biological Bases of Behavior: Neuroanatomy
The occipital lobe of the brain is located in the lower back portion of the cerebral cortex. Its primary function is the reception of visual information via the optic nerve. This visual information is then processed in the visual cortex region of the occipital lobe.

96. **A** Abnormal Psychology: Mood Disorders
Seasonal affective disorder (SAD) is a type of recurrent depression that is present during winter months. Its causes seem to be linked to shorter daylight hours, and it often disappears once longer days return. Some people find help in periodic exposure to sun lamps.

97. **D** Research Methods: Experimental, Correlational, and Clinical Research
The single-blind experimental procedure is one in which the participants don't know whether they belong to the experimental group or the control group. The purpose of this procedure is to lessen the placebo effect. A placebo is a nonactive treatment that is given to the control group. The placebo effect is the perceived effect of the treatment by the participants in the control group even though they are in reality taking a nonactive substance or treatment. Researchers need to account for the placebo effect when studying the effectiveness of a treatment.

98. **A** Treatment of Psychological Disorders: Treatment Approaches/Insight Therapies: Psychodynamic/Humanistic Approaches
Freud's technique of psychoanalysis assumes that personality is like an iceberg. Much of our personality is in the unconscious, which is below the surface and not seen. A psychoanalytic therapist attempts to uncover those hidden causes of behavior through questioning and probing.

99. **B** Learning: Classical Conditioning
Conditioned responses often become so powerful that a similar stimulus can elicit a similar reaction. In the case, the coil of rope appeared suddenly and looked enough like a snake to cause Carla to react just as she would have had she seen an actual snake. This phenomenon is known as generalization.

100. **C** Abnormal Psychology: Schizophrenic Disorders
Schizophrenia is a psychotic disorder characterized by disorganized and delusional thinking, disturbed perceptions, and inappropriate actions and emotions. Catatonic schizophrenia is most often characterized by immobility, but it can also manifest itself in excessive, purposeless movement.

SECTION II: FREE-RESPONSE EXPLANATIONS

Question 1

The following is an example of an experiment using classical conditioning
similar to the one that a typical student might create.

Let us assume that you want to train your pet guinea pig to squeak when his cage is opened. You would start out by opening the cage and immediately placing food in the food bowl. You are using an unconditioned stimulus, the food, to elicit an unconditioned response, which is the guinea pig's squeal at the sight of food. Over time, the guinea pig will learn to associate your neutral stimulus, that is, the opening of the cage, with food. This is the acquisition phase of classical conditioning. Over time, the guinea pig will become trained to squeal when the cage is opened even without the food being placed in the bowl. At this point you can say that the animal is conditioned. The former neutral stimulus, the opening of the cage, has become associated with the food enough so that the opening of the cage has become a conditioned stimulus. The squeal is now a conditioned response not to the food, but to the opening of the cage. Over time, the conditioning will generally weaken as the guinea pig learns that no food is forthcoming when the cage is opened. This weakening is called extinction, which is the reduction of a conditioned response over time.

Commentary on Question 1

Possible points: 10

- 1 point for each correct definition/explanation of a concept (6 points total)
- 1 point for each appropriate example for topics **A** through **D** (4 points total)

When completing this answer, the student should show evidence of a high degree of psychological knowledge concerning both classical conditioning and experimental design. This question asks the student to design an experiment using classical conditioning, so it is important that terminology related to experimental design be included. The student should clearly explain basic experimental procedures and might include terms such as *control*, *dependant variable*, and *independent variable*. He or she might also discuss placebo effects, confounding variables, and the double-blind procedure.

Other important terms should be defined as follows:

(A) An unconditioned stimulus (US) is a natural stimulus that automatically triggers a response. An example from Pavlov's experiment of a US would be food.
(B) A conditioned stimulus (CS) is a former neutral stimulus (NS) that becomes paired with a US and comes to trigger a conditioned response (CR). An example from Pavlov's work of a CS would be the bell.
(C) An unconditioned response (UR) is an unlearned naturally occurring response to a US. An example of a UR would be the dog's salivation at the sight of the food.
(D) A CR is a learned response to a previously neutral conditioned stimulus. The example in Pavlov's work of a CR is salivation.
(E) Acquisition is the initial stage in classical conditioning where the NS, such as the bell, becomes associated with a US, such as salivation, so that the NS becomes a CS.
(F) Extinction is the diminishing of a CR that can occur over time. This happens when a US does not follow a CS.

Question 2

Sample Response

Let's assume a person has just touched an object. The neural impulse would travel from a receptor in the hand to a sensory neuron. The impulse travels from the dendrite of the sensory neuron through the cell body down the axon of the sensory neuron to the synapse at the end of the axon. The impulse travels down the axon via a process known as the action potential. The action potential is caused by the interchange of positive and negative ions through the membrane of the axon. When the neural impulse reaches the synapse, it is passed across the synaptic gap via neurotransmitters. Neurotransmitters are chemical messengers that travel from one neuron to another. The impulse would travel via the peripheral nervous system, which is the part of the nervous system found in the limbs, to the spinal cord. The impulse would travel up the spinal cord to the brain. The spinal cord and the brain together form the central nervous system. The impulse would travel through the brain to the sensory cortex, which is located in the back of the frontal lobes of the brain. From there, the brain would decide an appropriate reaction and send an impulse to the motor cortex, which is located in the front portion of the parietal lobes. The motor cortex would direct an impulse back via the central nervous system and the peripheral nervous system to a motor neuron that is connected to a muscle. That impulse would tell the muscle what to do next.

Commentary on Question 2

Possible points: 8

- 1 point for each correct definition/explanation of a concept

When completing this answer, the student should show evidence of a high degree of psychological knowledge concerning both the structures and functions associated with the nervous system. In answering this type of question, it would be appropriate for the student to include a labeled diagram along with a narrative portion of the free response.

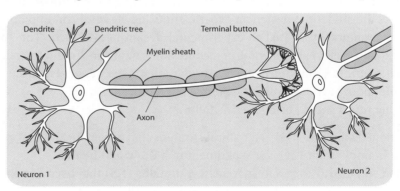

Neuron Structure

Students should note the following pieces of information:

- The path of a sensory nerve impulse would start at a receptor and travel to the dendrite of a neuron.
- The impulses would then travel through the soma to the axon and finally to the axon terminals, where it would cross the synaptic gap to the dendrite of the next neuron.
- The impulse would travel via the peripheral nervous system to the central nervous system and finally to the sensory cortex located in the brain.

- Then a motor impulse would leave the motor cortex and travel via the central nervous system back to the peripheral nervous system and finally to the muscle that it is intended for.

Students should also discuss the process of the action potential traveling through the axon and the transmission of neurotransmitters in the synaptic gap. Other important terms should be used in accordance with the following definitions:

(A) Neuron: a nerve cell. It is composed of the dendrite, the cell body, and the axon.

(B) Dendrite: the branching extensions of the neuron that send and receive impulses from other neurons.

(C) Axon: the long extension of the neuron that conducts the neural impulse to other neurons or cells.

(D) Action potential: a neural impulse. It is a brief electrical charge that travels down an axon, generated by the movement of positively charged ions in and out of the channels in the axon membrane.

(E) Peripheral nervous system (PNS): this system is composed of the sensory and motor neurons that connect the central nervous system to the rest of the body. The PNS is composed of two subdivisions: the autonomic nervous system, which controls glands and muscles of the internal organs, and the somatic nervous system, which controls voluntary skeletal muscles.

(F) Central nervous system (CNS): This system is composed of the brain and the spinal cord. The CNS sends nerve impulses from the body to the brain and the brain back to the body.

(G) Sensory cortex: a region of the brain located in the front of the parietal lobes that registers and processes body sensations. Body sensations reach the sensory cortex via the PNS and the CNS from the body.

(H) Motor cortex: the area of the brain in the rear of the frontal lobes that controls voluntary movement. Signals from the motor cortex travel to the body via the CNS and the PNS.